The Floater's Guide
to **MISSOURI**

by
Andy Cline

Copyright ©1992 by Falcon Press Publishing Co., Inc.
Helena and Billings, Montana

All rights reserved, including the right to reproduce this book or parts thereof in any form, except for inclusion of brief quotations in a review.

Library of Congress Catalog Card Number: 91-077724
ISBN: 1-56044-108-9

Manufactured in the United States of America

Falcon Press Publishing Co., Inc.
P.O. Box 1718, Helena, MT 59624

All text, maps, and photos by the author except as noted.
Cover Photo: by Charles Farmer

Printed on recycled paper

ACKNOWLEDGMENTS

I owe special thanks to two people who helped me find much of the information for this book that will help you enjoy floating in Missouri.

Joe Bachant, Fisheries Programs Coordinator for the Missouri Department of Conservation, and Bill Palmer, Director of Communications for the Department of Natural Resources, provided me with dozens of documents and books. Many of these you'll find useful, too. They are listed in the Appendix. One of these books, sadly, is no longer in print—*Canoeing in Northern Missouri*—published by the Department of Natural Resources in 1978. Bill Palmer generously allowed me to use much of the information in that book to prepare *A Floater's Guide to Missouri*.

The maps reproduced in *A Floater's Guide to Missouri* are based on County highway maps available from the Missouri Highway and Transportation Department. The Department sells these maps for 25 cents each, or a complete set for $25. This is the best map deal going, and I urge every serious floater—or any outdoorsman—to buy a set.

The Missouri Department of Conservation's book entitled Missouri Ozark Waterways was a valuable resource for pinpointing accesses and natural forms such a springs and caves. If you plan to float the Ozarks, get this book. It costs a modest $2 and has the best mile-by-mile descriptions of many Ozark streams.

Some of the statistics about the fifty streams in this book came from Missouri's Fishing Streams, a report by the Missouri Department of Conservation. Other books by the Department of Natural Resources that provided useful information included: Missouri Water Quality Report, Terrestrial Natural Communities of Missouri, and Geologic Wonders and Curiosities of Missouri.

Thanks to the Missouri Division of Tourism for supplying several of the photos in this book. Their *Missouri Travel Guide* was also a valuable resource.

Individuals who helped in various ways include: Andy Gerrard, expert outdoorsman; Don Clements, canoeing expert; Charlie Farmer, outdoors writer (he took the cover photo), and Kenny Kieser, outdoors writer. Thanks guys. And my special thanks to everyone at the Missouri Department of Conservation, the Conservation Federation of Missouri and the Department of Natural Resources. Without your vigilance, there'd be no streams to float.

CONTENTS

Acknowledgments
Introduction 1
How to use this book 4
Map legend 5
Water and skill classification 6
Safety and equipment 12
Rights of the floater 16
Logistics 18

THE FLOATS 20
Glaciated Plains 22
  1. Big Creek 24
  2. Chariton River 26
  3. Cuivre River 28
  4. Des Moines River 28
  5. Fox River 32
  6. Grand River 32
  7. Grindstone Creek 35
  8. Locust Creek 37
  9. Nodaway River 39
 10. One-hundred and Two River 41
 11. Platte River 43
 12. Salt River 45
 13. Thompson River 45
 14. Wyaconda River 48
Ozark Border/Ozark 49
 15. Big River 50
 16. Bourbeuse River 53
 17. Cedar Creek 54
 18. Sac River 56
 19. Loutre River 56
 20. Beaver Creek 58
 21. Big Piney River 59
 22. Black River 61
 23. Bryant Creek 63
 24. Bull Creek 65

25. Swan Creek 65
26. Courtois Creek 67
27. Huzzah Creek 69
28. Current River 69
29. Eleven Point River 72
30. Elk River / Big Sugar Creek 74
31. Flat Creek 77
32. Gasconade River 78
33. Indian Creek / Little Sugar Creek 81
34. Jack's Fork River 81
35. James River / Finley River 85
36. Meramec River 87
37. Moreau River 90
38. Niangua River 90
39. North Fork of the White River 94
40. Osage Fork of the Gasconade River 95
41. Pomme de Terre 98
42. Roaring River 98
43. Shoal Creek 102
44. Spring River 102
45. St. Francis River / Big Creek 105

Big River Region 107
46. Mississippi River 108
47. Missouri River 111

Mississippi Lowlands 113
48. Ditch #1 114

WATERSHED 116

FISHING 119

APPENDIX 126

v

LOCATION OF FLOATS

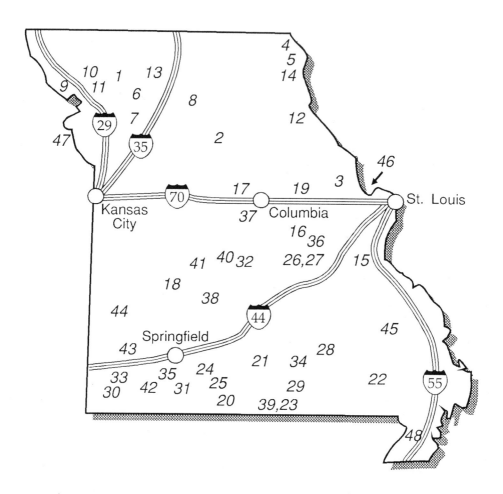

INTRODUCTION

The explorers Lewis and Clark followed an ancient highway into the Louisiana Purchase. The Missouri River led them west across what would become the state of Missouri and then northward into the high plains and the Rocky Mountains. And like any other highway, the Missouri River was a spur of a larger route called the Mississippi. Smaller routes broke off from the Missouri leading into the fertile land north of the river, the prairie southwest of the river and mountains to the south and east. Men who came later followed these streams to new lives.

You can, too. While you won't discover new lands or build a civilization where once there was wilderness, you will discover something within yourself. Modern man still needs wild places, not to tame or to exploit, but simply to be in. It is in these wild places we rediscover our connection to the Earth.

Water is the blood of the planet. And we are mostly water. There's no mystery to why we seek water for recreation after long days spent toiling in a cement environment. We boat. We sail. We fish. We ski. We swim. We skip stones.

And we float. We let the water coursing through the veins of the Earth carry us to adventures in a canoe, or raft or simply in an innertube.

We float in great numbers. There's no accurate count of how many

The relaxing sport of floating attracts the neophyte and experienced alike. Missouri Division of Tourism Photo.

Missourians float the state's 57,000 miles of rivers and streams. But a recent survey by The Gallup Organization for the Missouri Department of Conservation suggests an answer. In a random sample telephone survey, Gallup determined that forty-nine percent of respondents go floating in a canoe or jonboat on Missouri rivers and streams. Could this mean that half of Missouri's five million residents float—2.5 million people?

Yes. And the real figure is certainly higher when you add those who travel to Missouri for the scenic beauty and mild manner of our streams. If you've ever watched canoes launch on any summer Saturday on the Niangua River at Bennett Springs State Park, you know this figure is low. The Niangua flows bright with aluminum. This rush to the water plays on dozens of popular streams throughout the spring, summer and fall.

Why so popular? There are at least 2.5 million answers. I'll suggest just a few. First, without question, is that Missouri is home to thousands of miles of relatively unspoiled streams flowing calmly through prairies and mountains. Unlike some states where streams charge down hillsides like cavalry to battle, here the water is mostly gentle, offering just a few wild rides for thrill seekers. Beginners don't have to fear torrents to enjoy rugged scenery.

Missourians love to fish and our streams offer some of the best fishing in the state for popular species such as bass, trout, catfish and sunfish. In the Gallup survey, sixty-four percent said they enjoy fishing in Missouri's streams. And if you can name a better way to fish a stream than from a canoe, I haven't heard it. A canoe whisks you silently into deep pools and backwaters where fish rarely see an angler on the bank.

We love to swim in our streams. Summer is the most popular time to float. The uniform of the day is swim wear. And the floater who makes it to the end of the day without dunking in the cool, spring fed waters of an Ozark stream is an odd man out. According to the survey, forty-six percent enjoy swimming in Missouri's streams.

We love to party. When employees plan company outings, it often involves a float trip—fun for the workers and inexpensive for the employer. While it's certainly fun to float alone or with a small group, in summer the size of party flotillas rivals that of Navy battle groups. And they are often as loud, not with the roar of guns and bombs, but with the shouts of festive voices and the clanging and banging of neophyte paddlers having fun.

We love to get outdoors, especially if it's easy. There are few outdoor activities as easy as floating. You don't need much equipment. You don't need a canoe. You don't need lessons. You don't need a lot of money. All you need is that basic human desire to be in a wild place, to see wild things and to return home with pictures, memories and maybe a few fish for the skillet.

Let's talk more about easy. Suppose you've never floated before, or have taken a couple of trips with an organized group. First, you need to know where to float. This book, and other sources I'll cite, will tell you. You'll learn about the different types of streams in Missouri so you can choose the ones that fit your desires.

Next you'll need to know a little about handling a canoe. I've got you covered there, too. In fact, if you use this book and other readily available sources, you'll know everything you need to know to make that first solo or small-group trip like a pro.

Once you discover the sport of floating, you'll realize it's more than simply gliding along a stream lost in the moment. But it doesn't have to be. All it

You don't need a canoe to enjoy Missouri's streams. Dozens of commercial liveries rent canoes to individuals and groups throughout Missouri. Some outfits even offer camping and meals.
Missouri Division of Tourism Photo.

needs to be is whatever you choose to make it. Some floaters spend their lives happy to drift away in reverie on popular streams. Others seek bigger thrills. They look for whitewater rapids where they hurl themselves into the torrent in kayaks or rafts. Others go exploring. They choose to float unpopular streams with no services or conveniences and difficult access. Still others launch their tiny craft upon big water where they feel the power of rivers that drain a continent.

Floating is what you make it. It's what you want it to be. But there is one obligation. Open your eyes and see. Not just the scenery. Not just the wildlife. See the stream and what's happening there. See where man has interfered by clear-cutting a bank, dumping his refuse, spilling his chemicals or attempting to straighten a stream course.

Those 57,000 miles are not perfect. Only a fraction remain wild. These streams need you to open your eyes. Once you see, you'll know what to do. You'll know that floating is more than simply a sport. It's a call to pitch in and save the arteries of the Earth.

HOW TO USE THIS BOOK

Books can take you by the hand and lead you on fantastic journeys. I know this one will as you learn more about floating and enjoying Missouri's rivers and streams.

Floating is merely a vehicle to a larger enjoyment of the outdoors. And that enjoyment isn't complete without some background. This book is more than a simple description of rivers. Instead, you'll also learn a little about the history, politics, geography and wildlife that make up the regions and watersheds of the state.

You'll also learn a little more about rivers and streams throughout the state. While the Ozarks get all the publicity and the crowds, there are other regions of Missouri where clear streams meander through a spectacular landscape. And there are a few streams to the north that make up in fishing and adventure what they lack in scenery.

If you are a beginner, you'll find it helpful to read parts I and III before delving into the guts of book—the descriptions of various floats for 50 popular rivers and streams. In the first part, I discuss floating as an industry and as a recreation. You'll learn about the geographic regions of Missouri and how rivers in these regions differ. You'll also learn how you can get involved in the conservation of Missouri's watersheds.

Also in Part I, I'll discuss safety, equipment and the rights of floaters and landowners.

Everybody will find something of interest in Part III where I describe a watershed and how it works. I'll give you a few tips for fishing in Missouri's rivers and streams. It's some of the best fishing you'll find in the state, encompassing everything from catfish to trout.

Part II profiles 50 rivers and streams. Each listing describes the skill level, gradient and length. Also listed are the names of the appropriate U.S. Geological Survey topographic map quadrangles. A general description of the stream follows, giving you an idea of the sights you'll see and the pleasures or hazards you'll meet.

After you've read *A Floater's Guide to Missouri*, I urge you to check other resources before you float. It's a good idea to get U.S. Geological Survey topographic maps for any stream you plan to float. You can also get useful county maps that help you find access roads. The Missouri Department of Conservation also has maps and books available to make floating, fishing, and nature observation more enjoyable. You'll find details about these information sources throughout this book.

MAP LEGEND

Interstate Highways	═══(00)═══▷
U.S. Highways	═══(00)▬▬▬▷
State Highways/ Other Principal Roads (paved)	══(00)════▷
Unpaved Roads	=========
Map Scale	0 1 2 3 Miles

~~~~~~~~~~~~~~~~~~~~~~~
NATIONAL FOREST BOUNDARY

....
State Park or Wildlife Management Area Boundary

— · — · — · — · —
STATE BOUNDARY

River, Creek	～～
Access	▶
Dam	/
Rapids	||||
Waterfall	//
Spring	⌐
Cave	⌒
Fire/Lookout Tower	⊙

WATER AND SKILL CLASSIFICATION

Missouri isn't the wild west; it's the mild Midwest—a mildness reflected in its rivers and streams. In the west you'll find raging rivers where outfitters lead cringing tourists down whitewater torrents in rubber rafts. Missouri has nothing like that. Most of Missouri's streams are gently flowing ribbons. Boring? No way. What Missouri lacks in chilling excitement it makes up for in serenity.

A look at the gradient of Missouri rivers gives a clue to their gentle nature. Scientists classify streams by gradient, or the number of feet of elevation the stream drops per mile. A low figure indicates a gentle stream. Gradients are not constant. For example, the popular Current River has an overall gradient of 4.4—it drops an average 4.4 feet per mile. But the gradient for the sixteen-mile stretch from Montauk State Park to Akers Ferry is 8.7. This water is faster—more technical—than the stretch below Akers Ferry to the mouth of the Jack's Fork River which is 5. Below Jack's Fork River to Doniphan near the Arkansas border, the Current rates a calm gradient of just over three feet per mile.

Floaters also judge rivers and streams for difficulty on an international standard adopted by the American Whitewater Affiliation. There are six classifications expressed by class in Roman numerals:

Class I- EASY. Fast moving water with riffles and small waves. Few obstructions, all obvious and easily missed with little training. Risk to swimmers is slight; self-rescue is easy.

Class II- NOVICE. Straightforward rapids with wide, clear channels which are evident without scouting. Occasional maneuvering may be required, but rocks and medium-sized waves are easily missed by trained paddlers. Swimmers are seldom injured and group assistance, while helpful, is seldom needed.

Class III- INTERMEDIATE. Rapids with moderate, irregular waves which may be difficult to avoid and which can swamp an open canoe. Complex maneuvers in fast current and good boat control in tight passages or around ledges are often required; large waves or strainers may be present but are easily avoided. Strong eddies and powerful current effects can be found, particularly on large-volume rivers. Scouting is advisable for inexperienced parties. Injuries while swimming are rare; self-rescue is usually easy but group assistance may be required to avoid long swims.

IV- ADVANCED. Intense, powerful but predictable rapids requiring precise boat handling in turbulent water. Depending on the character of the river, it may feature large, unavoidable waves and holes or constricted passages demanding fast maneuvers under pressure. A fast, reliable eddy turn may be needed to initiate maneuvers, scout rapids, or rest. Rapids may require "must" moves above dangerous hazards. Scouting is necessary the first time down. Risk of injury to swimmers is moderate to high, and water conditions may make self-rescue difficult. Group assistance for rescue is often essential but requires practiced skills. A strong eskimo roll [for kayakers] is highly recommended.

Class V- EXPERT.
Class VI- EXTREME.

Rafting is another fun way to enjoy a float trip. Missouri Division of Tourism.

There is no Class V or VI water in Missouri. Class IV is rare even during flooding. Most streams in Missouri rate I or II.

The big rivers—the Missouri and the Mississippi—require a different set of classifications and precautions. You won't find rapids or stream-like obstructions. You will find strong currents, shifting sand bottoms, wing dikes and large-boat traffic.

But don't let this frighten you. The big rivers offer an experience unmatched by Missouri's smaller streams but require some experience and special precautions.

The Missouri Department of Natural Resources suggests these guidelines:

• Venture onto the big rivers only if you have canoeing experience. Both bow and stern paddlers should be able to control the canoe. At least one member of the party should have previous big-river experience.

• Don't venture onto the big rivers with fewer than two canoe parties.

• Always wear a life jacket. Big river currents are exceedingly deceptive and surprisingly strong. If you fall without a jacket, you may not be able to swim fast enough to catch up to the canoe as it floats down river.

• Canoe close to shore. In case of an accident, you'll be within easy swimming distance and out of the path of barges. Barge traffic, especially on the Mississippi, makes canoeing in the main channel dangerous.

• The big rivers are subject to strong winds that often negate the positive effects of current. Be prepared for hard paddling. Don't try to paddle across a hard wind. It's safer to paddle into the wind or get off the water until the wind subsides.

• Watch out for barges and other large boats. Barges throw huge wakes, or waves that can easily tip a canoe. When you see a barge coming, get out of the channel and move close to shore. Barges don't have brakes. They can't stop for you. Maneuver your canoe so you hit the wake head on. Never rest against the hull of a parked barge. The force of the current and the great displacement of a barge hull can suck a canoe and its paddlers under the hull. No rescue is possible.

- Avoid wing dikes and jetties. The submerged rocks and current displacement around these structures may swamp your canoe.
- Canoeists are welcome to pass through locks and dams. Avoid the face of the dam and the spillway. Travel only in the approved route into and out of the lock.

Tips for Novices

Paddling a canoe is easy. You dip the paddle into the water, stroke, and the canoe goes. To make the canoe go where you please, you should learn five basic strokes. These are: the forward stroke, the J-stroke, the back stroke, the draw stroke and the pry stroke. Each of these strokes propels the canoe in a different way.

The first and easiest stroke to learn is the forward stroke. As its name implies, it is the stroke you use to make the canoe go forward. This is the stroke you'll use for ninety percent of all your paddling.

Hold the paddle by the grip and the loom. Lean forward and dip the entire blade into the water toward the bow of the canoe. Pull the paddle toward the stern. Keep the blade perpendicular with the surface of the water. When you finish the stroke, pull the blade straight out of the water.

Twist the blade parallel with the surface of the water as you bring it forward for another stroke. This is feathering and it simply cuts the wind resistance on the blade. This makes a big difference in your stamina during a long, windy float.

There are certain twists and dips of the body that make this stroke more efficient. You'll learn these in time. For now, this simple forward stroke will send you down every river and stream discussed in this book.

The J-stroke is a correcting stroke for the stern paddler. The stern paddler controls the steering of the canoe. By virtue of the physics involved in paddling, the bow paddler applies power and the stern paddler applies direction.

You'll notice that a stern man paddling on the right will drive the canoe to the left—and vice versa. An inexperienced bow man can do little to correct this. So the stern man applies the J-stroke which kicks the stern back to a straight line.

Begin a J-stroke just like a forward stroke. As the paddle comes even with your hip, turn the blade outward and push it away from the canoe with your lower arm. The line of the stroke forms a J-shape, hence the name. An occasional and carefully applied J-stroke will keep your canoe tracking straight.

To stop a canoe, or back up, apply the back stroke. It is simply a forward stroke executed backwards. To stop the canoe, dip the paddle near your hip and push forward with your lower arm until the paddle breaks the surface. To move backwards, don't allow the blade to break the surface. In all strokes, allowing the blade to break the surface counteracts your stroke. This is useful when stopping a canoe, but it's quite inefficient when under way.

The draw and pry strokes allow you and your partner to make quick, dramatic turns. These strokes are useful when parking a canoe or when

THE PARTS OF A CANOE

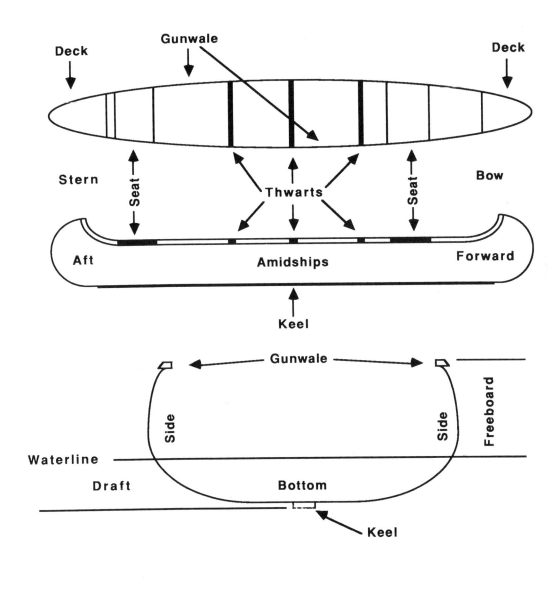

maneuvering or correcting course in fast water.

Both strokes move the canoe sideways. The draw stroke moves the canoe toward the paddle. The pry stroke moves it away from the paddle. To draw, lean outward, dip the blade parallel with the canoe and pull, or draw, the paddle toward you. To pry, hold the loom against the gunwale and push, or pry, the blade away from the side.

These five basic strokes will get you safely down any river or stream in Missouri.

Reading A Stream

Some Missouri streams are so lazy, you won't have to worry about choosing the proper course or avoiding obstacles. Most streams, however, offer some fast water and obstacles you'll have to maneuver through and around. You need the ability to read a stream.

Water is math. It adds up. Take certain observable facts, add a little river knowledge and sum is the safe route.

Water is power. Even on a small stream, the flow can create terrific pressure when gravity forces it over, under, around and through such obstacles as rocks, logs, fences, fallen trees, low-head dams and wing dikes. Your challenge is to find the safe route.

When water moves around objects it forms V-shaped lines. A rock obstructing the current, for example, would form a V pointing upstream—the rock at the point of the V and the water flowing around it forming the extending arms.

Most Missouri streams rate I—easy for beginners to handle. Missouri Division of Tourism.

Always avoid Vs pointing upstream. This means an object is blocking the current and could catch and tip your canoe.

Look instead for Vs pointing downstream. Water that flows safely around obstacles also forms a V. Think of them as open arms of safety. Avoid the point of an upstream V. Proceed into the safe arms of a downstream V. This simple method of reading a stream will carry you safely through most of the fast water in Missouri.

Other stream features to look for include eddies and standing waves. Eddies are calm areas behind a large obstacle such as a boulder. Eddies make good places to pull out of a fast current where you can safely and calmly check the rest of the fast water. You enter an eddy by making an eddy turn where the stern man steers the bow of the canoe into the calm water. As the fast water pushes the stern of the canoe downstream, the bow man powers the canoe into the eddy.

Standing waves indicate obstructions under the water. The waves may be gentle rollers indicating the obstructions are deep. Or they may be breaking waves indicating the obstructions are shallow. Always scout standing waves before proceeding.

THE PARTS OF A CANOE PADDLE

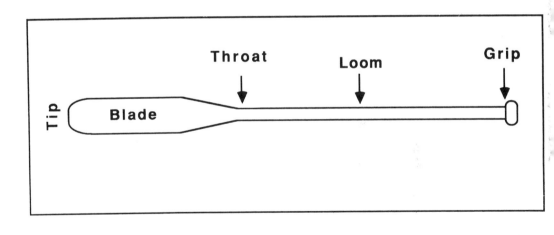

SAFETY AND EQUIPMENT

I took a group of Boy Scouts on a two-day trip down the Niangua a few years ago. The Niangua is a gentle stream. There are a few stretches of Class II rapids when the water is high. Most of the year it is Class I. It's a perfect stream for beginners and for adults leading a troop of enthusiastic Scouts.

Scouting rules require all boys who haven't earned swimming merit badge to wear a life jacket, also known as a personal flotation device. You should have heard their howls of bewilderment. Looking at that lazy stream, they wondered what could possibly happen to them that would require a life jacket. Superficially, it's a good question. When not in a high-water stage, the floater who "happens" into the Niangua can easily stand up and walk to the bank in most places. What's the big deal? They found out.

The Niangua is a popular stream. Hundreds of floaters bang and klunk their way downstream in aluminum rental canoes every summer day. The stream is one long ribbon of metal from June to September.

The members of a six-canoe party we came upon had been drinking heavily. Two women, who'd never canoed before, dumped at the end of every riffle. The Scouts, with much glee, fished them and their gear out of the stream several times. The women got a big kick out of being "rescued" and the Scouts got a kick out putting a few of their skills to work. Plus, young boys like to jump in the water.

But at one deep pool, one of the women panicked. The water was over her head. And in her alcoholic daze, she couldn't make her arms and legs propel her to safety. She went under once, twice, and then the Scouts got a rope to her and pulled her ashore. She came out of the water looking like a horror-stricken animal. Her cries and the awful contortion of her face scared the fire out of these brave boys.

I heard no more grumbling about life jackets.

A life jacket that fits like a vest, zips up the front and has a support collar for the head should be a standard piece of equipment in your canoe. And you should wear it anytime you venture into Class III water or above, or anytime that you're in water that's beyond your swimming ability. Be brutally honest with yourself about how well you swim. It could save your life.

Those are general guidelines. The best advice, however, is to wear your life jacket anytime you're on the water.

While a life jacket is essential, it's not the only safety equipment you should carry. Each canoe should have a bow and stern line of up to 15 feet. Be sure to use a synthetic, floating line that swimmers can easily see and grab.

This little story has another moral. Don't abuse alcohol on the water.

General safety guidelines

It's always a good idea, not to mention more fun, to float with a group of people. While floating alone along a wilderness stream is dreadfully romantic, it's only for the experienced who have a clear-headed notion of the dangers involved.

When your friends surround you, help is just moments away.

Always canoe with a plan, and let those left at home know what your plan is. Choose a group leader (rotate this job if you like) who'll blaze the trail. Make sure it's someone who can read a river and call back proper instructions to the rest of the group. Choose a strong swimmer and experienced paddler to bring up the rear. This person should watch over the group like a mother hen and come to the rescue when necessary. Never let the middle canoes wander ahead of the leader or fall behind the rear paddler.

Keep a comfortable distance between boats. A common accident on crowded streams is when one canoe flips and causes a chain reaction. When approaching a riffle, allow the canoe ahead to clear the fast water before you enter.

When dealing with rapids in water Class II and above, the leader should wait at the pool for the rest of the group to follow. This way the leader makes sure everyone gets through okay. And if a mishap occurs, he can direct the rescue effort.

If your companions tip, remember: people are more important than things. Make sure everybody is okay before you go rushing after boats and other gear.

This becomes especially important in cold water 50 degrees or below. Many of Missouri's streams are spring fed. The water can be rather cold year round. Be aware that the colder the water is, the quicker the body loses heat. Muscles become weak making it difficult to swim to safety.

There are elaborate charts to tell you just how long the average human can remain in water of various temperatures before muscle weakness occurs. Charts are one thing. Reality is another. If the water is 50 or below, figure on five minutes. Above 50 up to 60 degrees, figure on 15 minutes.

For those who wish to enjoy the full spectrum of Missouri floating, this information is vital. Winter is one of the finest times to paddle through the Ozarks. No crowds. Abundant wildlife. And great fishing.

Missouri's streams are pretty lazy. They wind through Ozark Mountains, across fertile lowlands and over rolling farm country. While you won't find the same exhilarating rides as in the west, will find beauty second two none.

You'll also find dangers.

Low-head dams are killers. Watch out for them. These low dams are usually visible during low water and covered during high water. Don't run low-head dams. Always portage around. The danger is swamping in front of the dam where the back flow will suck you under. The water pressure created by the dam is so overwhelming, you won't be able to pull yourself free. You will drown.

Watch out for obstructions in the water like fallen trees, barbed wire and log jams. If you can't see a clear path around an obstruction, then portage your canoe. Don't grab overhead limbs or other obstructions as you pass. This may cause your canoe to tip.

Safety on Missouri's streams is simply a matter of planning. If you're using an outfitter, the proprietor will know the stream conditions and will advise you on how to proceed. If you're outfitting your own trip, be sure to buy the latest maps available and call the Missouri Department of Conservation for more information.

Dozens of canoe liveries serve Missouri's popular streams. It's not necessary to own a canoe. A good choice for beginners is aluminum—easy to handle and maintain. Bass Pro Shops Photo.

Equipment

Besides rope and lifejackets, you'll also need a canoe. If you don't own one, don't worry. You'll find many outfitters in the Ozarks providing canoes, paddles, shuttle service and camp grounds.

You won't find many outfitters for streams outside the Ozarks.

Most outfitters rent the standard aluminium canoe. These are the war horses of Missouri streams. Aluminum canoes are inexpensive, light and built to take a pounding. And a pounding is exactly what they get from the thousands who rent them each year.

Aluminum canoes are low maintenance—a plus for the outfitter or budget-conscious owner. But aluminum dents easily. And because aluminum stretches, dents are usually permanent. If you like rugged and don't care about looks, aluminum is for you.

Canoes made of fiberglass, plastic and Kevlar will also stand up to the rocky bottoms of Ozark streams. In fact, canoes of these materials will glide over rocks easier than aluminum. Some plastic canoes, like those made by Coleman, will flex and give. Hit an exposed rock with aluminum, and you may tip. Hit one with plastic and you'll likely bounce off or glide over.

Consider the weight of a canoe before buying. While weight means little on a typical Missouri stream, it means a lot when hefting a canoe onto a car-top carrier or portaging around an obstruction.

Aluminum and fiberglass can be heavy or light depending on the design of the canoe. Plastic canoes are usually heavy. Kevlar canoes, like those made by Wenonah, are the lightest of all. Some 18-foot models weigh less than 45 pounds. Kevlar is also tough and stands up well to rocks and gravel.

Some canoes have keels—a spine that runs the length of the hull. A keel is useful for open-water paddling because it helps a canoe track straight in the wind. Canoes with keels are slightly harder to turn than canoes without keels.

A canoe with no keel is the best choice for streams. They are easy to turn and less likely to tip if you get broadside to an obstruction.

Unless you plan to motor in Missouri's streams, avoid canoes with square sterns. These are hard to paddle and turn. You may find a small electric or gas-powered motor handy on some of the northern streams, the bigger rivers or on the wide sections of some Ozark streams if you plan to do a lot of fishing.

For this book, let's assume you prefer to paddle. Choosing a paddle isn't complicated, but you do have to keep a few points in mind.

First, a paddle should "fit" properly. Fit is largely a matter of personal taste. Some say a short paddle will exhaust you. A long paddle is awkward to use. Start with a paddle that reaches your chin. Also choose a paddle with a wide blade. A wide blade has a bigger bite in the water and makes paddling easier. An 8-inch wide blade is a good choice.

Paddles come in wood, aluminum and other synthetic materials. You can spend as much a few dollars for a set of three, or more than $100 per paddle. Oh, always buy three and take them all with you. It's no fun getting caught up the creek without a paddle.

If you intend to camp—and carry your gear with you in the canoe—invest in some good dry bags. Household garbage bags just don't cut it. Garbage bags fall prey to every stray limb. One hole and it's shot.

One of the agreeable things about camping by canoe is you can have a wilderness experience and still take everything with you. Canoes hold a surprising amount of gear. I like to take my camp bed, a behemoth I can't possibly take on an overnight hike. My floating partners and I also like to take such items as: dutch ovens, camp chairs, coolers with food and other refreshments, large tarps, and tons of fishing gear. Can't carry all that stuff into the wilderness on your back. But in a canoe...no sweat.

Follow these two rules when loading a canoe: 1) Balance your load in the middle of the canoe; and 2) Don't tie the load in.

The urge to tie in a load of gear is enormous. Resist. If you tip, you want the load to float free. This makes recovering the canoe easier. If you want to know the true meaning of helpless, sink a loaded canoe in a deep hole in the middle of no where.

For expensive gear like cameras, buy float bags.

There are oodles of gear and gadgets you can get as you advance. But for 99 percent of all floating in Missouri, the basics outlined here are all you need. Add to this list: drinking water, snacks, sun screen, insect repellent and a wide-brimmed hat.

RIGHTS OF FLOATERS AND LANDOWNERS

While several of Missouri's most popular streams flow through state or federal lands, most streams flow through private land. And in Missouri, if a landowner owns both sides of the stream he also owns the stream.

This doesn't mean landowners have the right to control the stream completely. This doesn't mean you have to seek permission to float. You may float along any navigable river or stream in the state. But you may not have the right to stop, camp, put in or take out just anywhere you please.

Confrontations between landowners and floaters are rare today. Most people recognize the recreational value of Missouri's streams. And they recognize that it is the floater and the landowner who are the ones most likely to get involved protecting streams through the Streams for the Future program administered by the Missouri Department of Conservation.

When you plan a float trip, first look for public access areas provided in state parks, federal lands or access points developed by the Missouri Department of Conservation. You may also put in and take out at bridge crossings or other highway right-of-ways. All other access points will be private property. Get permission before you use a private access. Don't be surprised if the landowner charges a small fee. This is well within an owner's rights. Some

If you're planning to camp, first look for commercial camping areas, camps in state parks and national forests. Tracker Marine Photo.

In Missouri, if you own both sides of the stream, you also own the stream bed. But floaters do have the right to float across private land and camp below the high-water line. Missouri Division of Tourism.

landowners set up livery and camping businesses along Missouri's streams.

You won't find as many public access areas or private liveries north of the Missouri River as you'll find in the Ozarks. This region just doesn't attract as many floaters. But that's changing. The Missouri Department of Conservation reports increasing interest in northern streams. These streams are less crowded. Be aware that landowners in the north are not used to floaters like landowners in the Ozarks.

If you plan to camp, first look for commercial camping areas, camps in state parks, or other state and federal lands. You may, however, camp or portage on land, sand, or gravel bars below the high-water line on streams that cross private land.

While more unlikely today, you may still encounter a testy landowner who doesn't want you camping or stopping on his land—even on the lands below the high-water line. The way to handle this is be polite and move on.

The best way to ensure continued good relations between floaters and landowners is to treat the land as if it's yours. It's hard to believe, but people still need reminding: Don't litter; don't open or close gates without permission; don't harass farm animals; do seek permission; and thank the landowner. You can further help relations by getting involved in the Missouri Stream Team program. This program encourages individuals and landowners to work together to protect and restore streams and watersheds.

It's okay to camp or prepare a picnic on gravel bars below the high-water line. When in doubt, be sure to ask permission. Andy Cline Photo.

THE LOGISTICS OF FLOATING

Floating can be as simple or complicated as you please. For the beginner, the best way to start is with an outfitter. You'll find listings for outfitters within many of the river descriptions and in the appendix of this book.

Using an outfitter is not costly. Most rent canoes for under $30 a day—even less in the off season. This fee usually includes shuttle service. Add a small camping fee and you've got a complete trip.

It works this way: Suppose you want to float the Niangua, a gentle and popular stream in the Ozarks. You simply call an outfitter in that area and make arrangements for a canoe and camp site. After meeting at the outfitter's campground, you'll be shuttled to the put-in. Then you'll float back to camp. And if you want a multiple-day trip, you'll continue to another appointed take-out where the outfitter will pick you up and take you back to camp. Easy. And the cost is low.

The next step, once you're hooked, is to buy your own canoe. The outfitter is still useful because he provides a shuttle and camping while you get used to your new canoe.

Soon the day comes when you're ready to go it alone, perhaps on a river that has few services. Let's look at the logistics of floating as they affect how you get from point A to point B and back again.

You can launch a canoe into most Missouri streams where public roads cross or run parallel. Bass Pro Shops Photo.

Shuttling

What do you do with your car? That's probably the toughest decision for beginning floaters, especially if you didn't think about this before you arrived at the stream. On most of the rivers and streams described in this book, you can't simply go downstream a ways, then turn around and go back. You have to reach point B, then you have to get back to A with the canoe.

When there's only two of you in one car, the best way to handle this is either pay an outfitter to shuttle you or to move your car from point A to B.

The more adventurous and trusting among us don't worry about it and simply take off. Once they reach point B, they hope to find a kindly local, or another floater, who will take them back to their car. I've done this and it makes me nervous. I much prefer to float with an outfitter either providing a shuttle or moving my truck.

With two vehicles, the problem is solved. Take one vehicle to the take-out first. Load the canoes on the other vehicle and head for the put-in.

Camping

I'd rather camp by canoe than any other means. Like backpacking, you're out in the wilderness and must carry what you need to survive. Like camping by car, you take all kinds of goodies.

I've been known to take in a canoe (at one time, mind you): a dutch oven, a grill, camp bed, chairs, fishing gear, clothes and food for five days, cooler with beverages, drinking water, cameras, cook tarp, tent and many other bits of civilization. And it all fits! There's no need to want for anything.

But be sure you've packed properly. Balance your load in the middle of the canoe and in relation to the weights of the two canoeists. You don't want the canoe riding up at the bow or stern; this makes maneuvering in fast water difficult, or impossible.

Pack what shouldn't get wet in good river bags—heavy duty PVC bags made for canoeing. If you don't have these, use heavy-duty garbage bags and close them with twist-ties. If something can get wet, leave it out of a dry bag.

What if you tip? Some say you should tie your load into the canoe. Others say this is asking for trouble. I prefer a middle course. Tie in only what you can't live without. I always tie in my camera and my tackle box. I leave everything else loose.

Be sure to bring plenty of extra plastic bags for hauling out trash. Be a low-impact camper. Don't burn plastic or aluminum in your campfire. Carry these out with you. Extra bags also give you have a place to put litter you may find while floating. As astounding as it seems, some people still throw litter into Missouri's streams. I've never understood how they can do this after seeing the natural beauty of these watersheds. Some screw must be loose. You will find litter. If you can, please pick up after these slobs. It sets a good example.

Timing your float

In this book you'll find short float trips and long adventures. How long these trips last depends on three factors: speed of the current, skill of the floater, and your personal goal.

Generally, for floating and no fishing, plan no more than six to eight miles per day on a slow stream and eight to fifteen miles per day on a swift stream. If you're fishing, subtract three to five miles from these figures for a normal six-hour day. If you're able and willing to put in ten-hour days, you can cover more territory.

THE FLOATS

Missouri means "people with big canoes," an Algonquian word given to the Indians living near the mouth of the Missouri River. That's fitting. It was water, and man's ability to travel upon it, that created the state of Missouri and its role in westward expansion.

The French traveled up the Mississippi to discover new lands. Americans traveled up the Missouri to open the west. Today, Missourians travel these waters and the smaller rivers and streams to discover the natural beauty of the state.

Floating is big business in Missouri. Floaters are tourists who keep the cash registers ringing in towns like Eminence, Caufield, Bourbon, Sycamore, and Pineville that border the state's most popular float streams. In this book you'l find more than 100 businesses listed that rent canoes for about $30 per canoe per day. And while we're floating, we also fish, swim, camp and have picnics How much money are talking about? According to figures published by th Missouri Department of Conservation (MDC), all forms of recreation on th popular Meramec River, for example, had an annual value of $27 millio dollars, or $55,000 per mile. Even the Missouri River, thought unpopular and dangerous, brings in $3,500 recreational dollars per mile.

Floating is big politics. The popularity of Missouri's streams for floating and the desire to see them protected is one of the forces behind the Missouri Stream Team program where groups or individuals adopt a stream to protect and care for it.

The idea grew from Missouri's first Rivers and Stream Conference in February 1988. The purpose of the conference was to bring conservation professionals and interested citizens together to find a way to protect our stream resources. The Federation, a large, statewide group of individual conservationists, devised Stream Team to be an active agent. With expert help from the MDC, groups can adopt streams and conduct surprisingly extensive projects to care for them.

"Stream Teams learn how to survey their adopted stream," says an MDC report entitled Streams for the Future. "A survey booklet provides examples of the best and worst conditions to help [teams] rate their stream's health in each of the following areas: stream banks, riparian zones, watershed conditions, stream channels, water quality, aquatic habitat and scenic values."

The evaluation of these characteristics then points the way to action either for the group, the Federation or the MDC. Such action can be as simple as picking up litter or as involved as planting willows to stabilize eroded banks.

Because 93 percent of the land that Missouri's streams flow over is private property, the MDC is working with landowners to show them how to protect streams. Such a high percentage of private ownership makes the landowner an important link. With landowner cooperation, Missouri's streams have a future. Without landowner cooperation, there is no future.

The MDC Landowner Cooperative Program seeks to show landowners that stream care is good business by using state resources and manpower to help them correct problems and avoid future problems.

We inherited many of today's problems. Farmers and developers began channelizing streams around the turn of the century in the false assumption this would end flooding. But what happened? Flooding got worse and a new problem occurred—soil erosion. This led to even more drastic measures, such as dumping automobile bodies and other large refuse into streams to stabilize banks.

Today's programs help correct the sins of the past with cooperation never seen before among diverse interests.

Pollution remains a problem—for everybody, not just floaters—because 75 percent of Missouri's drinking water comes from streams.

And as we grow in numbers, there's yet another problem—one not likely to leave us. We are quite literally loving our streams to death. We set upon them by the millions in motor boats, rafts, canoes, innertubes and other craft. We fish, we hunt, we float, we hike, we do hundreds of activities centered around our streams. No matter how much we love them, great numbers of people using our streams is hard on the resource.

You'll find a diverse collection of issues surrounding our streams, just as you'll find a diverse topography. Of the 50 streams described in this book, each has a personality born of its region.

Missouri's terrain varies from flat plains to rough hills. The lowest elevation is 230 ft. along the St. Francis River in the southeast, and the highest point is 1,772 ft. at the summit of Taum Sauk Mountain in the St. Francois Mountains south of St. Louis.

Missouri has several geographic regions: the Ozark Highlands, the Ozark

Border, the Glaciated Plains, the Big River Region, the Mississippi Lowlands, and the Western Prairie.

This book describes floats in five of these six regions.

The Ozarks and Ozarks Border are hilly areas with large forests and small farms. Most of Missouri's popular streams flow through these two regions. The Glaciated Plains are the repository of glacial till sediments that make the northern half of Missouri—a prized agricultural region. The Big River Region is the flood plains of the Missouri and Mississippi rivers. And the Mississippi Lowlands is Missouri's bottomland country of swamps and farms growing corn and cotton.

At the time of settlement, the flatter parts of the plains region were covered with prairie grass that reached heights of 7 ft. The more dissected parts were covered with hardwood forests. In the Ozarks an oak and hickory forest prevailed, with short-leaf pine intermixed. The Mississippi Lowlands had a forest of bald cypress, tupelo, and sweetgum. You can still see some of these natural areas protected in state parks and other state lands listed in this book.

While you float Missouri's streams you'll also see wildflowers such as orchids, water star-grass, and watercress. You'll see abundant wildlife if you're quiet and observant, such as whitetail deer, wild turkey, beaver, muskrat, otters, raccoons, and birds such as king fishers, wood ducks and bald eagles. You'll see natural landscapes that include limestone bluffs, loess deposits, caves and sink holes.

And after you've seen these things, I hope you'll give the Conservation Federation a call and ask how you can help make sure another generation sees these same things.

GLACIATED PLAINS

The Missouri River cuts the state in two. South of the river are four distinct geographic regions. But most people simply think of this area as the Ozarks. North of the river is a single land of low rolling hills and farms. It is the glaciated plains.

Most people don't think of the plains as a place to float. They dream first of the Ozarks and its clear, spring-fed streams. Too bad. The plains offer something the Ozarks have lost—true adventure.

Popularity breeds access. The more people who come to an area to float, the more campgrounds, canoe outfitters, convenience stores, and tourist shops you'll find. The wild Ozarks just aren't as wild as they used to be. Sure, you'll still be floating through wild, scenic country. You just won't have to work very hard to enjoy it.

Work? Yes. Some floaters still look for areas where access isn't so easy, where it takes a little effort and some guts to tackle a stream. If you want to get away from the crowds, if you want to work a little harder for your pleasure, look to the glaciated plains.

You won't find roaring rapids here. What you will find are lazy, uncrowded streams—most of them with gradients less than three-feet-per-mile—teaming with fish and other wildlife. And if you simply can't imagine a float without clear streams and limestone bluffs, guess what—the glaciated plains have a few of these, too.

Fishing is the most popular activity on the streams of the glaciated plains. These streams flow gently southward with few rapids. Andy Cline Photo.

The name glaciated plains comes from an event more than one million years ago—the advance of a Pleistocene glacier. The southern boundary of this ice sheet was the Missouri River. Above it, the land spent tens of thousands of years under the weight of glacial ice. South of the Missouri River, the land remained exposed and slowly eroded into the Ozarks we know today.

The glaciated plains reflect this age. The streams here form a trellis pattern on the land flowing almost uniformly north to south reflecting the drainage of the great ice sheet. The glaciers deposited up to 200 feet of sediments in this area forming the rich farmland we know today.

One type of sediment deposited is called loess—the sandy material prevalent along many of the norther rivers, including the Missouri, that causes the steep muddy banks of this region.

Loess is a loose-surface sediment originally formed by wind action during ice age. The wind drove it into deep piles along the bluffs of the northern rivers. Some deposits in Missouri are as deep as 150 feet. The gray or yellowish color of the deposits is caused by the presence of iron oxide minerals. Loess contains silt-size grains, mostly of quartz but also of clay minerals, feldspar, mica, hornblende, and pyroxene. Carbonate minerals are sometimes abundant. It is highly porous yet quite stable.

Farmers who settled this area in the early 1800s recognized the value of the rich, glacial soil. It's responsible for making Missouri one of the top agriculture states in the nation.

To further agriculture interests, Missourians began channelizing the northern streams around the turn of the century. The idea was to control flooding and increase the acreage of farm land. It had the opposite effect. Flooding often got worse. And if that wasn't enough, channelization also intensified erosion because farmers often left no trees or brush in the stream corridor to stop the run-off.

This is why today we perceive the northern streams as muddy ditches. Sadly, many of them are.

But this is changing. Farmers, conservationists, and developers are beginning to work together to save streams from further destruction. Such programs as the Missouri Stream Team (sponsored by the Conservation Federation of Missouri and the Missouri Department of Conservation) are making a difference. Today, you can float many miles of pleasant streams north of the Missouri River.

Be sure to keep watch for wildlife as you float the glaciated plains. The habitat of this area is perfect for whitetail deer, squirrels, bobwhite quail, pheasant, skunks, beavers and other small mammals.

FLOAT 1 BIG CREEK

Region: Glaciated Plains
Difficulty: I
Quadrangles: Pattonsburg County
Maps: Harrison, Daviess
Statistics: Drainage Area, 400 sq. miles; Permanent Flow: Twenty-five miles
Put in: Highway 69 bridge south of Bethany, or bridge at Bridgeport for one-day trips
Take out: Bridge at Bridgeport

The float: To better understand the ravages of channelization in northern Missouri, all you have to do is float Big Creek. Here is one of the few unchannelled streams that still winds its way through the rolling hills toward the Grand River.

Along Big Creek you can still see what many northern streams have lost—natural riparian habitat and a functioning watershed. It's a great stream for watching wildlife, including: deer, turkey, beaver, and birds like owls and hawks.

The stream is gentle and floatable when water levels are normal to above normal.

Big Creek begins with the confluence of West Fork Big Creek, East Fork Big Creek and Little Creek near Bethany in Harrison County. It is a gentle stream with a few riffles and log jams. You can float nearly all of its twenty-five miles. Be prepared to portage around some of the log jams.

A good one-day float begins at the access at the Highway 69 bridge south of Bethany. The landscape rolls and the stream banks are wooded most of six miles from Bethany to Bridgeport. There is an access at the bridge at Bridgeport for a short day trip.

For a longer day trip, continue on six more miles to the bridge at Highway 69. The bank is steep here. You'll need ropes to hoist your canoes out of the water. Along this section the stream is less wooded and you'll see more agriculture.

For a two-day trip, continue on eight more miles to the third Highway 69 bridge at Pattonsburg. The Grand River is ten miles farther. See the description of the Grand River for access areas.

FLOAT 1 *BIG CREEK*

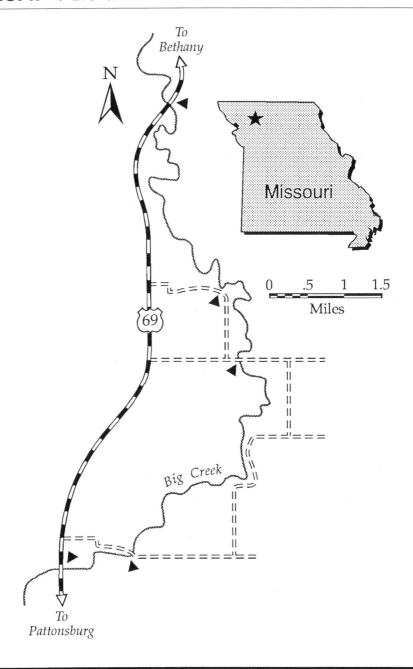

FLOAT 2   *CHARITON RIVER*

Region: Glaciated Plains
Difficulty: I
Quadrangles: Centerville
County Maps: Adair, Putnam, Schuyler
Statistics: Drainage Area 3,040 sq. miles; Permanent Flow 124 miles
Put in: The dirt road off County Road Z or at the Rebel's Cove Wildlife Access. You can also enter the stream from the Mock Bridge on the dirt road between County Roads Z and N
Take out: The Highway 136 bridge in Livonia

The float: The Chariton is an enigma. According to an MDC recreational value survey, the Chariton ranks 25th among thirty-eight popular rivers and streams, but in the future it's expected to post the largest gain in worth as a recreational river.

Why? The 1982 survey report speculates: "Recent acquisitions by the Department of Conservation for river access and other public uses may explain part of the respondents' optimism." Two such access areas include the Archangel Access southwest of Lancaster on Highway 136 and Rebel's Cove Wildlife Area, both in Schuyler County.

The survey also shows the Chariton suffers problems common to most northern Missouri streams: channelization, water withdrawals, poor land use, intensive agriculture, and pollution.

You can float the entire length of the Chariton from the Missouri-Iowa border to the Missouri River when water levels are adequate. The most natural part of the river is the section running from the Iowa border, past Rebel's Cove to the town of Livonia. The stream banks have mostly been left forested.

The land rolls here making it poor cropland but excellent habitat for deer and turkey.

The Chariton is a good river for catching catfish. The water levels in the Chariton fluctuate because of discharges from the Rathbun Dam in Iowa. Fishing is best when the water is rising.

Unimproved access areas to the Chariton are difficult—especially in wet weather when you need a four-wheel-drive to negotiate the dirt roads. You can begin your float either from the dirt road off County Road Z or at the Rebel's Cove Wildlife Access. You can also enter the stream from the Mock Bridge on the dirt road between County Roads Z and N.

There are two more access areas along dirt roads before reaching Livonia, twelve miles from Rebel's Cove. At Livonia, exit at the Highway 136 bridge.

You can float the Chariton to the Missouri. For more information on access areas, check the Discover Outdoor Missouri Map published by the MDC (See Appendix).

FLOAT 2 CHARITON RIVER

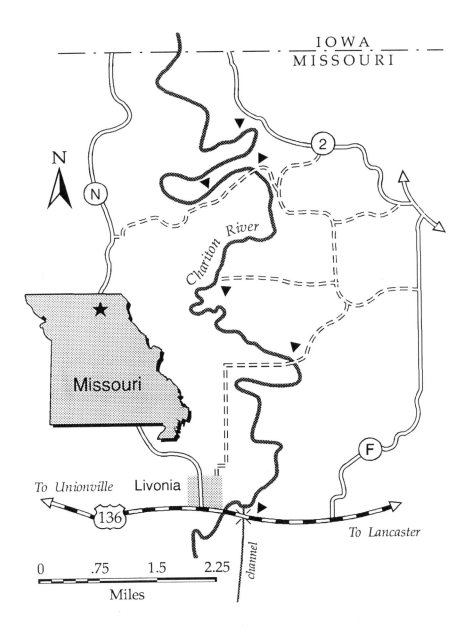

FLOAT 3 *CUIVRE RIVER*

Region: Glaciated Plains
Difficulty: I
Quadrangles: Silex, Elsberry, Warrenton, Troy, Maryknoll, Winfield
County Maps: Lincoln
Statistics: Drainage Area 1,230 sq. miles; Permanent Flow 34.5 miles
For more information: Cuivre River State Park, call 314-528-7247.
Put in: Highway 67 bridge
Take out: Highway 47 bridge

The float: For an easy and scenic float in north Missouri, you can't beat the Cuivre River and the four-mile stretch between the the MDC Riggs Ferry Access at the Highway 67 bridge and the Highway 47 bridge.

Part of this route takes you by the 6,251-acre Cuivre River State Park, an area of rugged hills and forest. This is an area known as the Lincoln Hills, an uplift that escaped the crushing weight of glacial ice that flattened much of northern Missouri. The area looks much like the Ozarks.

Interesting natural features within the park include springs, sinkholes and natural ponds. You'll see landscapes as different as 150-year-old stands of white oak and prairie grasslands.

Wildlife using the park include deer, turkey, and birds such as the pileated woodpecker.

The park includes thirty-one miles of hiking trails plus camping.

Prehistoric man also camped in the area as ago as 12,000 years. The park contains evidence of campsites, villages and ceremonial grounds.

FLOAT 4 *DES MOINES RIVER*

Region: Glaciated Plains
Difficulty: I
Quadrangles: Croton, Argyle, Wayland, Keokuk
County Maps: Clark
Statistics: Permanent Flow within Missouri twenty-nine miles
Put in: Battle of Athens State Historic Site on Country Road CC
Take out: MDC Alexandria Access, two miles downstream from confluence of Mississippi on the right

The float: The Des Moines River is the major artery separating Iowa from Missouri. The stream bed is expansive, meandering and bordered by limestone bluffs lush with forest and brush in the upper reaches. As the Des Moines approaches the Mississippi River past St. Francisville, agriculture rules the landscape.

The Des Moines River offers an excellent one- or two-day float. There are plenty of sandbars and beaches for camping and picnics. Be sure to keep an eye on the water level. Red Rocks Reservoir in Iowa controls the stream flow which may fluctuate a few feet over short periods.

FLOAT 3 *CUIVRE RIVER*

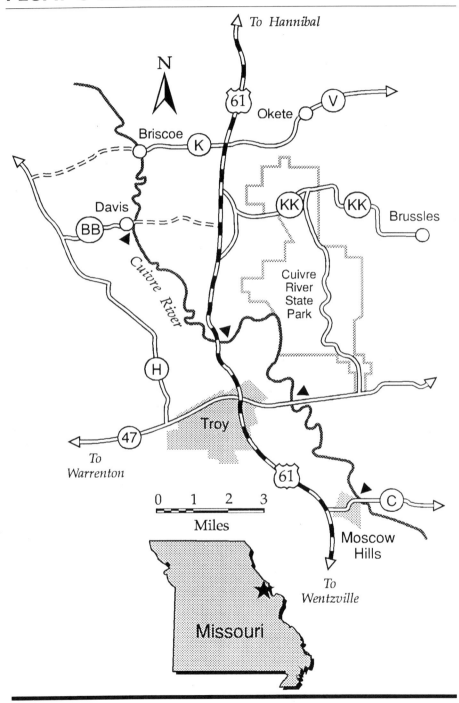

Floaters who take their fishing poles catch walleye and sauger on the rivers and streams in northeast Missouri, including the Des Moines River, Salt River and Wyaconda River.
Missouri Division of Tourism Photo.

Begin your float at Battle of Athens State Historic Site on Country Road CC in Clark County. This site commemorates the northernmost battle of the Civil War west of the Mississippi River—fought between Union Troops and the Missouri State Guard. The site offers a campground and picnic area.

There's an MDC access just above St. Francisville at 12.5 miles on the right past the bridge.

For a two-day trip, or a one-day trip on the lower river, continue on fourteen miles to the confluence of the Mississippi River. The MDC Alexandria Access is two miles downstream on the right.

For more information about Battle of Athens State Historic Site, call 816-877-3871.

FLOAT 4 DES MOINES RIVER

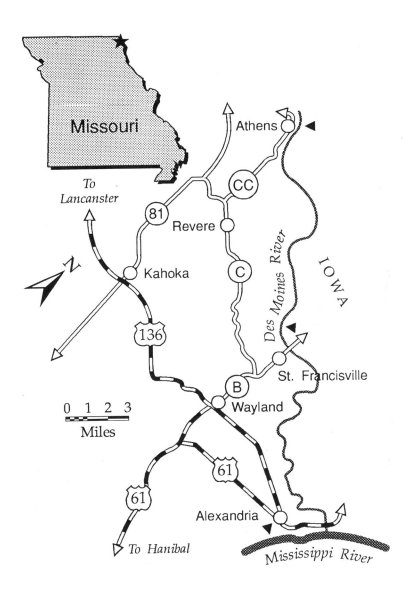

FLOAT 5 *FOX RIVER*

Region: Glaciated Plains
Difficulty: I
Quadrangles: Anson, Kahoka, Medill
County Maps: Clark
Statistics: Drainage Area 502 sq. miles; Permanent Flow twenty-four miles
Put in: MDC access at the Fox State Forest
Take out: Highway 81 bridge

The float: The Fox River is Missouri's sleeper. Because it flows through the hilly farm country of extreme northeastern Missouri, most people assume it's muddy and uninteresting.

Not so. The Fox River will surprise you. It is a clear stream with a gravel bottom much like streams in the Ozarks. Sections of the lower river offer a scenic float like the Ozarks, plus there is a good smallmouth bass fishery.

An MDC survey of recreational value ranks the Fox thirty-sixth of thirty-eight popular rivers and streams. This low ranking, however, shows more ignorance of the Fox than a true reflection of its recreational value. Certainly there are problems on the Fox, including channelization, intensive agricultural development and poor land use.

But to see the Fox for the natural wonder it is, put in at the MDC access at the Fox State Forest off County Road NN two miles west of Highway 81. It's about an eight-mile float to the Highway 81 bridge.

This is a small stream. In summer, be prepared to drag your canoe over shallow riffles and gravel bars. This is a perfect time for anglers to wade and fish for smallmouth bass in the deep pools. For a smooth run, float in the wet seasons. Because of channelization to the north, the Fox is not a pleasant float during high water when it turns swift and muddy.

FLOAT 6 *GRAND RIVER*

Region: Glaciated Plains
Difficulty: I
Quadrangles: Grant City, Darlington, Pattonsburg, Gallatin, Chillicothe, Utica, Hale
County Maps: Worth, Gentry, Daviess, Livingston, Carroll, Chariton
Statistics: Drainage Area 7,900 sq. miles; Permanent Flow 384 miles
Put in: MDC Access on County Road H east of Darlington
Take out: For multi-day float, Vaughn Tract Access south of Gallatin on Highway 13

The float: The Grand River is popular with the residents of northern Missouri. It is the region's largest watershed and longest river. This gentle river attracts many boaters, anglers and an increasing number of floaters.

On an MDC survey of recreational value, the Grand ranked last among the

FLOAT 5 *FOX RIVER*

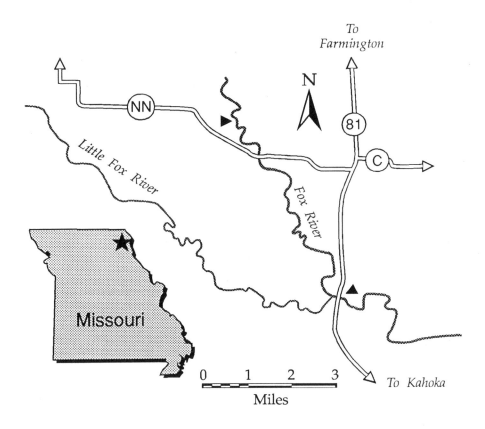

state's thirty-eight most popular rivers and streams. The survey indicates, however, this popularity will rise in the near future. The Grand offers excellent fishing for catfish. There are few obstacles for floaters. And you'll find plenty of sandbars for camping and picnics.

These characteristics make the Grand a good choice for adventuresome floaters who want to make a multi-day trip on a northern river.

You won't find the services and outfitters available in the Ozarks, but you also won't find the crowds.

The Grand River winds its way south toward the Missouri River in the heart of the north's agricultural land. The Grand suffers from channelization in some areas. Other problems, according to the MDC survey, include: intensive agricultural use (some fields come right to the bank), water withdrawals for irrigation, sand and gravel dredging, and shoreline development.

Floating the Grand is certainly a pleasant experience for the hearty canoeist, but it is also a study in the ravages of human development. You'll still find forest some areas with old cottonwoods and sycamores.

FLOAT 6 GRAND RIVER

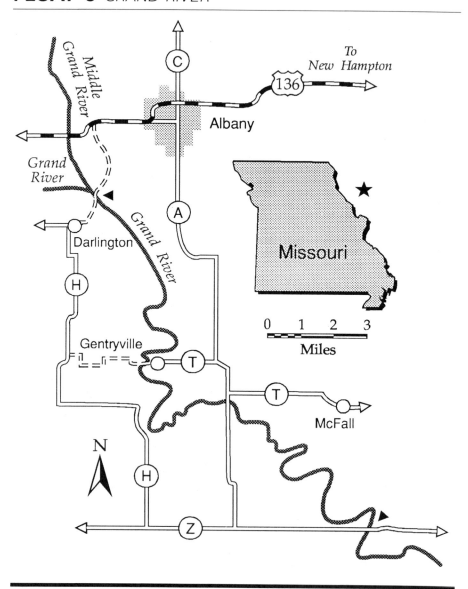

The Grand River winds its way south toward the Missouri River in the heart of the north's agricultural land. The Grand suffers from channelization in some areas. Other problems, according to the MDC survey, include: intensive agricultural use (some fields come right to the bank), water withdrawals for irrigation, sand and gravel dredging, and shoreline development.

Floating the Grand is certainl a pleasant experience for the hearty canoeist, but it is also a study in the ravages of human development. You'll still find forest some areas with old cottonwoods and sycamores.

Begin your float in Gentry County at the MDC Access on County Road H east of Darlington. Your first day will take you ten miles to the MDC Koger Access on County Road Z west of Pattonsburg.

Continue on from Koger Access six miles to the Green Access on Highway 69 south of Pattonsburg. This stretch also makes an excellent one-day float.

From Green Access, it's twenty miles downstream to the Wabash Crossing Access at Highway 13 near Gallatin. This is too long a float to handle in one day for average canoeists. Expect to make this run in two days by camping on a sand beach.

From Wabash Crossing Access, it's five miles to the Vaughn Tract Access south of Gallatin on Highway 13.

Lower stretches in Livingston County flow by the Fountain Grove Wildlife Area, an excellent place to view wildlife.

FLOAT 7 GRINDSTONE CREEK

Region: Glaciated Plains
Difficulty: I
Quadrangles: Maysville, Winston, Pattonsburg
County Maps: Dekalb, Daviess
Statistics:
Drainage Area: 324 sq. miles; Permanent Flow: 0 miles
Put in: the gravel road off County Road C just northeast of Gridley
Take out: Country bridge off the gravel road south of Weatherby. For longer runs, the Highway 6 bridge two miles downstream

The float: An interesting ten-mile float is Grindstone Creek, a small tributary of the Grand River. The Grindstone twists its way northward—rare for streams in the north which usually form trellis patterns on the landscape heading south to the Missouri River.

Thick stands of trees and brush line most of the route forming a green tunnel through farm country.

During periods of high water, you can easily float this gentle stream from near Gridley to just south of Weatherby in Dekalb County. What little current there is won't cause you problems. You will, however, encounter log jams along the twisting course. Be prepared to portage around these obstacles.

Begin your float at an access on the gravel road off County Road C just northeast of Gridley. Several county bridges on gravel roads cross the Grindstone one mile, three miles and eight miles downstream. Each offers access for shorter runs.

FLOAT 7 GRINDSTONE CREEK

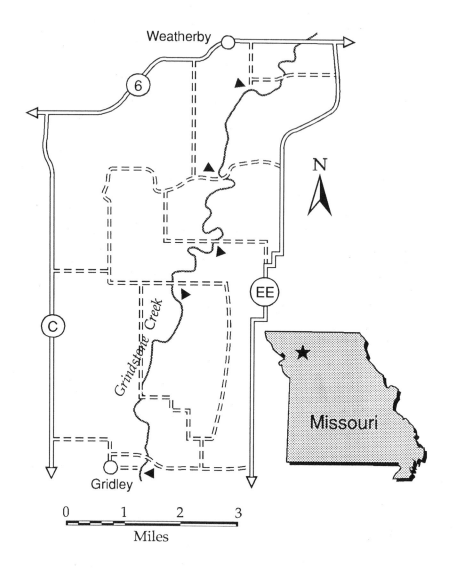

Take out at the county bridge off the gravel road south of Weatherby. For longer runs, take out at the Highway 6 bridge two miles downstream. The Grand River is sixteen miles from the Weatherby take-out.

There are no services or public areas along this route. Be sure to pack waterproof boots for portaging around log jams.

You'll find plenty of deep holes with catfish, bass, bluegill and walleye along many streams of the glaciated plains. Andy Cline Photo.

FLOAT 8 *LOCUST CREEK*

Region: Glaciated Plains
Difficulty: I
Quadrangles: Hale, Sumner, Brookfield
County Maps: Linn, Chariton
Statistics: Drainage Area 631 sq. miles; Permanent Flow 7.5 miles
For more information: Pershing State Park, 816-963-2299.
Put in: Highway 36 bridge. Within the state park for a shorter trip
Take out: It's best to take out in the park. Two access areas are below the park, one at ten miles and the other at twelve miles

The float: Locust Creek offers one of the last looks at a naturally meandering northern Missouri stream with mature bottomland forest. But that's not all. You can also see areas of natural prairie, all but vanished from the state.

Like most small creeks in the north, Locust Creek suffered channelization from Iowa over much of its length. The lower stretches remain wild, especially the section flowing through Pershing State Park. The park offers floaters a glimpse of mature cottonwoods and birch in a rich bottomland that floods often. The park is a memorial to General John J. Pershing, leader of the American Expeditionary Forces in World War I, who grew up in nearby Laclede.

FLOAT 8 LOCUST CREEK

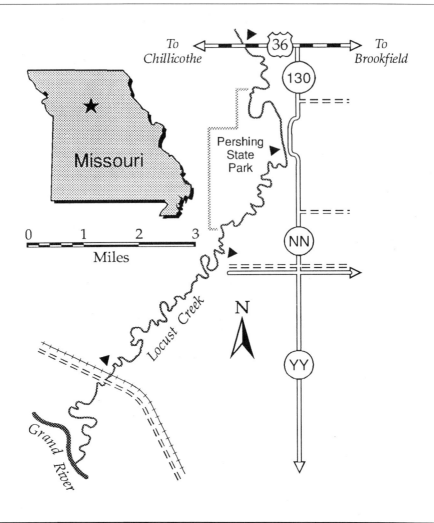

Above the bottoms in the forest, you'll find mature silver maple, river birch and several varities of oak. You'll also discover the ostrich fern, a rare find. According to the Department of Natural Resources (DNR), the area "retains the quality of an undisturbed, presettlement landscape..."

The 1,040-acre prairie area is the largest wet prairie left in Missouri. There were once more than seven million acres of prairie in northern Missouri, according to the DNR. This native grassland includes such plants as cordgrass, water smartweed, big bluestem, compass plant, and prairie blazing star.

Besides natural beauty, Pershing State Park also preserves the history of Native Americans. You'll find Indian mounds in the park that date back nearly 1,000 years.

It's best to float Locust Creek in the spring when wet weather keeps water levels up. You find lots of sandbars for picnics and rest stops.

Begin your float at the Highway 36 bridge. You'll cross into the state park at 2.5 miles.

You can launch within the state park for a shorter trip. Watch for obstructions in the stream at the abandoned bridge. You may have to portage.

It's best to take out in the park. Two access areas below the park, one at ten miles and the other at twelve miles, are usually impassable during wet weather.

FLOAT 9 NODAWAY RIVER

Region: Glaciated Plains
Difficulty: I
Quadrangles: Amazonia, Forbes, Maitland
Country Maps: Andrew, Holt
Statistics: Drainage Area: 1,780 sq. miles; Permanent Flow: fifty-two miles
Put in: by the bridge on county road A two miles west of Fillmore
Take out: access .5 mile after Smith Creek enters from the right

The float: The Nodaway River is a favorite fishing stream in northeast Missouri. Residents regularly catch hefty stringers of channel catfish along its entire length. The Nodaway is also an excellent stream for floaters.

The headwaters are near Lake Anita State Park in Iowa. The river enters Missouri five miles north of Clearmont along Highway 71. The Nodaway is channelized over most of it's length. But south of the Holt County line, where the river forms the boundary among Holt, Nodaway, and Andrew counties, the channel flows normally to the Missouri River just north of St. Joseph.

The Nodaway has steep, muddy banks due to large deposits of loess characteristic of streams across the Glaciated Plains. It flows slowly, offers floaters plenty of opportunity to fish or simply enjoy the scenery.

Much of the scenery is rolling farmland. The section within the Honey Creek Wildlife Area is wooded and wild.

The Department of Natural Resources identifies a six-mile section, beginning near Fillmore and passing through Honey Creek Wildlife Area, as the best floating.

Put in by the bridge on county road A two miles west of Fillmore. This is a steep access. You may need ropes to lower the canoe.

The Nodaway meanders through low, rolling hills and farmland. You'll find a few riffles and many long pools.

At 3.8 miles, you'll cross under the Interstate 29 bridge. At 5 miles, the Nodaway becomes the western boundary for the Honey Creek Wildlife Area.

Take out is at an access .5 mile after Smith Creek enters from the right. The access is along a gravel road 6.1 miles from put in. There is a county bridge about another half mile down stream.

For a longer float, or overnight trip, continue to the Missouri River, more than five miles beyond the Smith Creek access. You'll find excellent camping spots on sandbars. Take out at the Monkey Mountain Wildlife Area, in Holt County, off highway U. Enter the Missouri River and continue downstream 1.5 miles to the Nodaway Island access provided by the Missouri Department of Conservation.

FLOAT 9 NODAWAY RIVER

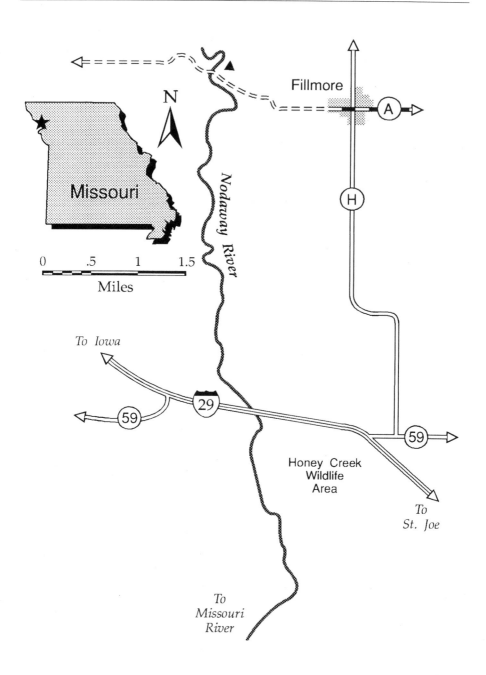

FLOAT 10 ONE HUNDRED AND TWO RIVER

Region: Glaciated Plains
Difficulty: I
Quadrangles: Savannah, St. Joe North
County Maps: Andrew, Buchanan
Statistics: Drainage Area: 781 sq. miles; Permanent Flow: 70 miles
Put in: Route E bridge east of Savannah.
Take out: Last take out, Mitchell Avenue twin bridges

The float: The One Hundred and Two River flows south from Iowa and is floatable over most of its seventy miles. Several sections have been channelized. But much of the river still flows naturally.

A particularly enjoyable twenty-mile float parallels the Platte River from Savannah to St. Joseph through Andrew County and Buchanan County. Put in at the Route E bridge east of Savannah. The banks of the One Hundred and Two River are not as steep and some streams in the Glaciated Plains. But the banks are still quite muddy and put-ins and take-outs will be difficult except at developed areas.

The One Hundred and Two flows through rolling farm country. You'll discover rock outcroppings and ledges. There are many sand and gravel bars for camping or fishing for catfish. A popular fishing method here is setting bank lines baited with prepared stinkbaits. You can also catch catfish by drifting stinkbaits under snags and blow-downs with a rod and reel.

There are two county bridges crossing within the first four miles. The Rock Quarry access, owned by the Missouri Department of Conservation is five miles downstream. This eight-acre area has a concrete boat ramp for easy access. The run just before this area is fast in high water. Watch for a drop-off at the bridge when the water is low.

You'll cross under the highway 169 bridge about eight miles downstream. A nearby gravel road makes a good access.

Steep banks at the Cook Avenue bridge, fifteen miles downstream, make access difficult. You'll need to lift your canoe with ropes to put in or take out.

The final take out is twenty miles downstream at the Mitchell Avenue twin bridges. The One Hundred and Two River joins the Platte River just south of this access.

You can make several other easy trips on the One Hundred and Two River because the Missouri Department of Conservation owns three more access points north of Savannah. The 715-acre Happy Hollow Wildlife Area in Andrew County has 5.4 miles of river frontage, making a float within this area a pleasant one-day trip. The ninety-two-acre Hadorn Bridge access in Andrew County has one mile of river frontage plus a camping area. The thirteen-acre Black Oak access in Nodaway County has .25 mile of river frontage.

FLOAT 10 ONE HUNDRED AND TWO RIVER
FLOAT 11 PLATTE RIVER

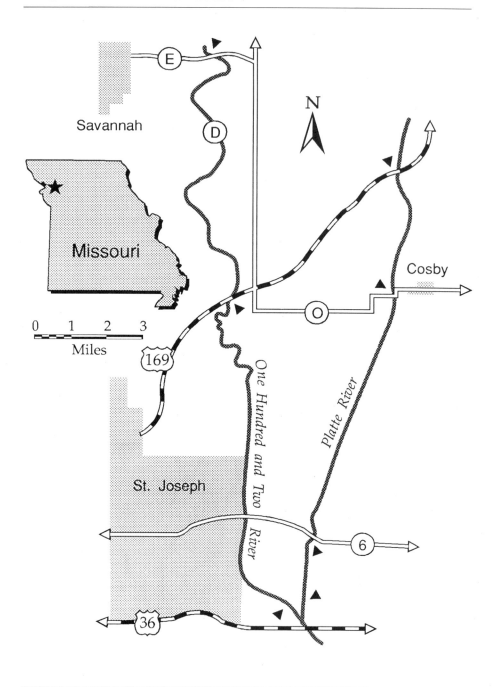

FLOAT 11 PLATTE RIVER

Region: Glaciated Plains
Difficulty: I
Quadrangles: Edgerton, Smithville, Leavenworth
County Maps: Andrew, Buchanan, Platte, Worth
Statistics: Drainage Area: 2,440 sq. miles; Permanent Flow: 138 miles
Put in: MDC Rochester Falls Access on highway 169
Take out: Twin Bridges access

The float: A distinct difference between streams of the north and south are the trellis patterns of the northern streams. These streams flow almost uniformly south creating a parallel trellis pattern on the landscape. Streams in the south meander around the Ozark hills haphazardly.

The Platte parallels the One Hundred and Two River for most of its distance from Iowa to near the Missouri River. The Platte enters the Missouri twenty miles north of Kansas City. Because the Platte runs between the urban centers of Kansas City and St. Joseph, it is a popular stream; not for floating, but for fishing.

Anglers fish the Platte for catfish and rough fish such as carp and buffalo. The Missouri Department of Conservation manages nine access areas along the Platte making it one of the easier northern streams to float. The banks of the Platte are mostly sand not mud, an added bonus.

Put in at the MDC Rochester Falls Access on highway 169. It's three miles to the next access at the route O bridge and another six miles to the access at the highway 6 bridge. Eleven miles from put in is the Twin Bridges access common to the final access of your float on the One Hundred and Two River.

You can float the Platte for all of its length in Missouri when the water is up. The stream has long pools and several shallow areas where you'll have to portage.

Also consider these areas when planning a float. There's a pleasant six-mile float from the Worth County bridge on highway 246 east of Sheridan to the MDC Keever Bridge Access in Nodaway County.

There are several MDC managed access points in Platte County where the Platte meets the Missouri River. They range from five to seven miles apart making an easy day trip between any two access points: 1) one-acre Union Mill with .02 mile of frontage is five miles to; 2) twenty-one-acre Ringgold access with .3 mile of river frontage and camping is eleven miles to; 3) ten-acre Sharp's Station with .5 mile of river frontage is eight miles to; 4) the highway 371 bridge in Platte City which is five miles to; 5) eleven-acre Humphrey access with .4 mile of river frontage and camping is seven miles to; 5) eleven-acre Schimmel City access with .3 mile of river frontage, camping and a concrete ramp.

Floating the north country is a real adventure. You'll find fewer services, less access, more portages, and difficult put-ins and take-outs. But you'll also find uncrowded floating and surprisingly pleasant scenery. Tracker Marine Photo.

FLOAT 12 *SALT RIVER*

Region: Glaciated Plains
Difficulty: I
Quadrangles: Stoutsville, Florida, Joanna, Center, New London, Hannibal, Barry, Bowling Green
County Maps: Ralls, Pike
Statistics: Drainage: 2,900 sq. miles; Permanent Flow: seventy-four miles
Put in: County Road H
Take out: MDC Indian Camp Access

The float: The Clarence Cannon Dam interrupts what was once an excellent float stream in north Missouri. But you can still enjoy the stretches below the dam. There's excellent fishing here for catfish, sunfish and bass.

The Salt River ranks 19th in popularity in a recreational value survey conducted by the MDC. The MDC expects the Salt's recreational value to grow. Problems with the Salt, according to the survey, are intensive agricultural use, poor land use, pollution, channel modification, and impoundments.

The Salt's stream banks are largely sand and gravel. You'll find numerous limestone bluffs. There are lots of sand and gravel bars suitable for camping and picnics. The water is surprisingly clear for a northern Missouri stream.

You can canoe the entire fifty miles from the dam to the Mississippi River. But there are several, pleasant one-day trips available closer to the dam.

Put in at County Road H and canoe twelve miles to the MDC Indian Camp Access. For a slightly long trip, continue on three more miles to the County Road V bridge.

The area grows huge catfish. Take along a stout pole and plenty of live bait (such as crawdads) and stinkbaits. Use heavy line and float your bait into deep holes around heavy cover with a bobber.

FLOAT 13 *THOMPSON RIVER*

Region: Glaciated Plains
Difficulty: I
Quadrangles: Lamoni, Iowa-Missouri
County Maps: Harrison
Statistics: Drainage Area: 2,200 sq. miles; Permanent Flow: sixty-three miles
Put in: Dirt road east of route O near the Iowa border
Take out: Dirt road east of route O.

The float: To the extreme north is a pleasant four- mile float on the Thompson River.This is one of the last unchannelized segments of this river which flows south from central Iowa to the Grand River.

The Thompson River is a large stream, but there are times during the summer when some sections are too low to float. And most of the channelized sections are less than scenic.

Put in off the dirt road east of route O near the Iowa border. This road may

FLOAT 12 *SALT RIVER*

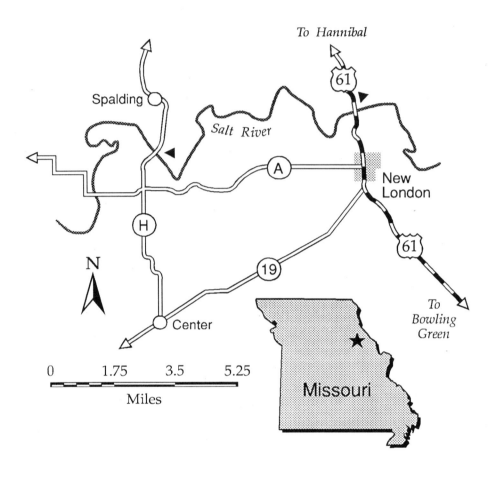

be muddy during the spring. After a heavy rain, you may need a four-wheel-drive vehicle.

The river is mostly wild and tree-line through this section. Except in high water, you'll find plenty of sandbars for picnics and camping. Two miles downstream is another possible put-in off a gravel road north of route O. Again, the road may be too muddy for anything but a four-wheel-drive vehicle after a rain.

Three miles downstream, where the stream makes a sharp curve, is an old mill dam. Watch for riffles in the curve. Take out at the dirt road east of route O. Again, this road my be muddy after a rain. The stream bank here is steep.

From here the channelized stream flows south to the Grand River. While the scenery is what you'd expect from a channelized stream, the fishing for catfish is pretty good.

FLOAT 13 THOMPSON RIVER

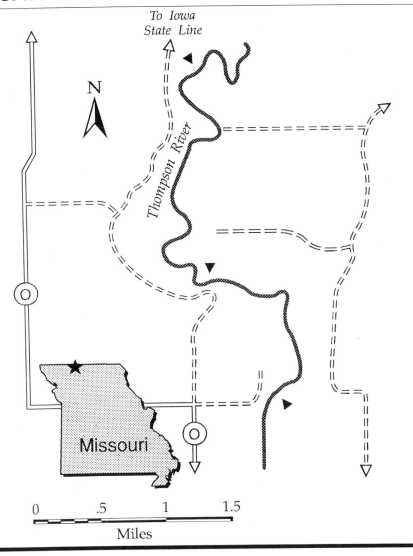

FLOAT 14 *WYACONDA RIVER*

Region: Glaciated Plains
Difficulty: I
Quadrangles: LaGrange
County Maps: Lewis
Statistics: Drainage Area: 462 sq. miles; Permanent Flow: twenty miles
Put in: highway 61 bridge north of LaGrange
Take out: Route B bridge north of LaGrange

The float: Although the northern sections of the Wyaconda are channelized, the seven-mile section near the Mississippi River offers a float as scenic and wild as any in the Ozarks. This is one of the north's best floats.

The Wyaconda flows south from Iowa into northeast Missouri. In the lower sections, you'll see long rock ledges, limestone bluffs, waterfalls and an abundance of wildlife including deer, turkey and beaver.

Put in at the highway 61 bridge north of LaGrange. Steep banks make this a difficult access. One-half mile downstream is an exposed ledge of Burlington limestone bedrock. Watch for a drop in the river with riffles.

There is another drop in the river with riffles 1.5 miles downstream along a rock ledge to the right. The main channel flows to the right around an island four miles downstream. There's another island .5 mile farther on with a drop in the river and riffles.

FLOAT 14 *WYACONDA RIVER*

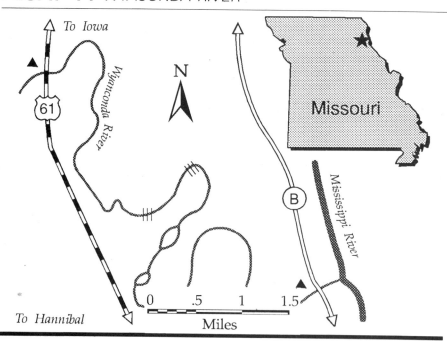

48

OZARKS/OZARK BORDER

The Ozarks have the glamour. You simply can't beat clear, spring-fed streams and rugged Ozarks hills as a calling card. Most of the canoeing, rafting and kayaking enjoyed in Missouri happens in the Ozarks.

All this activity makes the region easy to visit. With a phone call, you can arrange everything from a simple canoe rental to an entirely outfitted week including camping, cooking, fishing and just about any other convenience.

The Ozarks is an interesting region. While there are some areas of uplift, most of the Ozarks is an eroded table land—the hills formed by millions of years of water slowly carrying the soil away to the Gulf of Mexico. This erosion carved spectacular landforms, from limestone bluffs to the exposed boulders of the Shut-ins country.

The Ozarks and Ozarks Border covers most of the southern half of Missouri and has an average elevation of about 1,000 ft. The region is famous for more than 4,000 caves and many large springs.

In southern Missouri, streams flow away from the crest of the Ozark highlands in all directions, unlike the streams of the north that flow almost uniformly south to the Missouri River or east to the Mississippi. Ozark streams are fed by a complex network of springs. The discharge is relatively stable throughout the year.

The Ozarks is home to the first National Scenic Riverway—the Current and Jack's Fork rivers in the eastern Ozarks. The Mark Twain National Forest and other state forests cover large tracts of the Ozarks.

Settlement through the 1800s established a subsistence farmer-woodsman economy, much like Appalachia in its cultural traits. The cultural influences of this time are still reflected in the Ozarks. It's a popular region to visit for crafts, art, and handmade goods of all kinds.

From 1880 to 1920, lumbering companies exhausted the best of the Ozark timber and moved to new territories. This led to soil erosion and a loss of wildlife. Many former loggers turned to agriculture on hardscrabble farms. Modern timber management has replaced much of this loss.

There's a modern spin to the old Ozark ways and you can see this in Branson at the Silver Dollar City amusement park where actors recreate life in the 19th century Ozarks. For a more modern appeal, Branson offers many country music shows. In fact, Branson can rightly be called the new home of country music as yearly new big-name stars open theaters here.

The streams of the Ozarks offer something for every floater. You'll find quiet, gentle streams easy enough for any beginner. And you'll find a couple of streams tough enough for the most experienced. This is the best region to begin your life as a floater. It's easy to start here because so many outfitters take care of everything. Plus the ruggedness of the hills, the abundance of wildlife, and the excellent fishing draw you back again and again.

FLOAT 15 BIG RIVER

Region: Ozark Border
Difficulty: I
Quadrangles: Bonne Terre, Cedar Hill, Fletcher, House Springs, Pacific, Richwoods, Tiff, Vineland
County Maps: Jefferson, St. Francois, Washington
Statistics: Drainage: 955 miles; Permanent Flow: 117.5 miles
Put in: Two-day float - access north of Bonne Terre on the road that follows the Missouri Illinois railroad tracks; one-day float - the MDC Jeremiah Blackwell Access
Take out: Washington State park
Area outfitters:
• Cherokee Landing, Rt. 4, Box 303, Bonne Terre, MO 63628, 314-358-2805;
• Ford's Canoe Rental, Cedar Hill, MO 63016, 314-285-2564
For more information: about Washington State Park, call 314-586-2995.

The float: The Big River, which is close to St. Louis and suffering the effects of nearby lead mining, might seem a river best avoided. People who know the

FLOAT 15 BIG RIVER

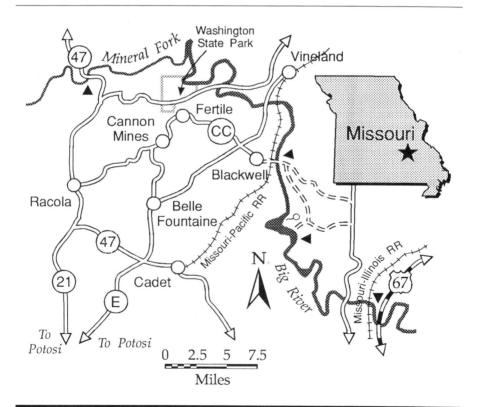

Most Missouri streams are gentle, rarely registering a difficulty rating over class II. Tracker Marine Photo.

river, however, rate it highly as a float stream, according to the MDC survey of recreational value. The Big River scored 8.4 out of 10 for recreational value and placed eighteenth out of thirty-eight popular Missouri rivers and streams.

Pollution, intensive recreational use and shoreline development continue to be problems, according to survey respondents.

Like the Bourbeuse, the Big River flows slowly and gently toward its confluence with the Meramec River. The section near Washington State Park is the best for floating, including the Mineral Fork.

Washington State Park offers canoe rental and shuttle service making it a good base for a Big River float trip. The park also has a camping area and cabins for rent.

The area around Washington State Park is rugged bluff country well forested with evergreens and mature hardwoods. You'll also see limestone glades which are openings of bare rock in the forest. You'll find prairie grasses and wind-flowers in these desert-like glades.

This area and the 1,415-acre park was home to the prehistoric Middle Mississippi people. You can still see the petroglyphs they carved in the stone near the southern boundary of the park between 1,000 and 1,600 A.D.

Put in at the access north of Bonne Terre on the road that follows the Missouri Illinois railroad tracks. From here, it's a two-day float to Washington State Park twenty miles downstream. For a one-day run, put in at the MDC Jeremiah Blackwell Access just east of Blackwell.

To run the Mineral Fork, put in at the County Road F bridge. It's a little more than a fourteen-mile trip to Mammoth Bridge where you'll find an MDC access.

Many Ozark streams run shallow in summer and require very little equipment to float. Bass Pro Shops Photo.

FLOAT 16 BOURBEUSE RIVER

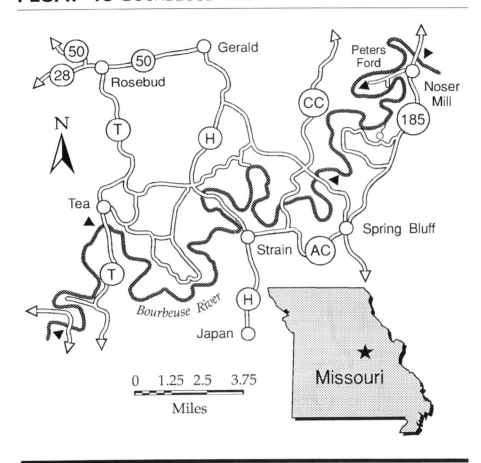

FLOAT 16 BOURBEUSE RIVER

Region: Ozark Border
Difficulty: I
Quadrangles: Gerald, Oak Hill, St. Clair, Union
County Maps: Franklin
Statistics: Drainage: 808 sq. miles; Permanent Flow: 106.5 miles
Put in: In the spring when the water is high, at the Highway 19 bridge
Take out: MDC Tea Access off County Road T.
Area outfitter: (also see Meramec River)
•Devil's Back Floats Rt. 1, Box 236 Leslie, MO 63056 314-484-3231

The float: The Bourbeuse River snakes its way through the Ozark Border region to its meeting with the Meramec. According to Oz Hawksley, the man who explored and cataloged the streams of the Ozark region for his book Missouri

Ozark Waterways (see appendix), the Bourbeuse winds 100 miles within Franklin Country, but covers a distance of only twenty-seven linear miles.

The MDC recreational value survey ranks the Bourbeuse high—7.1 out of 10. Compared to the other thirty-eight rivers and streams it ranks 20th. Survey respondents say intensive agriculture, poor land use, and shoreline development are the top threats to the river.

The Bourbeuse is not as clear as other rivers in the area, but the landscape remains mostly wild. Plus you'll find plenty of good fishing opportunities for bass. Look for them in the pools near cover such as fallen logs or weeds.

In the spring when the water is high, put in at the Highway 19 bridge and float ten miles to the MDC Tea Access off County Road T. For multi-day trips, continue on to the MDC Mill Rock Access another seventeen miles downstream. The area past Mill Rock is better floating in the summer. Put in at Mill Rock for a week-long trip to the MDC Reiker for Access forty-seven miles downstream.

FLOAT 17 *CEDAR CREEK*

Region: Ozark Border
Difficulty: II and III
Quadrangles: Millersburg, Millersburg SW
County Maps: Boone, Callaway
Statistics: Drainage Area: 230 sq. miles; Permanent Flow: twenty-one miles
For more information: National Forest Service headquarters in Rolla, at 314-364-4621.
Put in: County Road WW
Take out: County Road Y bridge twenty miles from put-in

The float: Cedar Creek flows through the only area of the Mark Twain National Forest north of the Missouri River. These federal lands offer a wealth of camping and hiking opportunities for the floater.

Cedar Creek rarely has enough water for canoeing except in the spring after a period of rain. It can be a wild ride past limestone bluffs and woody obstacles as the stream winds its way toward the Missouri River. You may have to portage around log jams and other obstacles, especially if the water is fast. This is not a stream for beginners. You should have one experienced floater per canoe.

You can make an excellent twenty-mile two- or three-day trip on this stream beginning at County Road WW. This is a treacherous access. The next twelve miles offer an exciting ride past tall bluffs, through fast chutes and around tight bends.

Past the twelve-mile mark, Cedar Creek is a little less wild, although you should still use caution. You'll see more agricultural activity.

Take out at County Road Y bridge twenty miles from put-in.

Below this take-out, Cedar Creek begins to slow down as it meanders through the bottomlands toward the Missouri River thirteen miles further on.

Although Cedar Creek flows through the Mark Twain National Forest, much of the land is privately owned. You may camp below the low-water line on private land, althought it's still best to get permission.

FLOAT 17 CEDAR CREEK
FLOAT 18 SAC RIVER

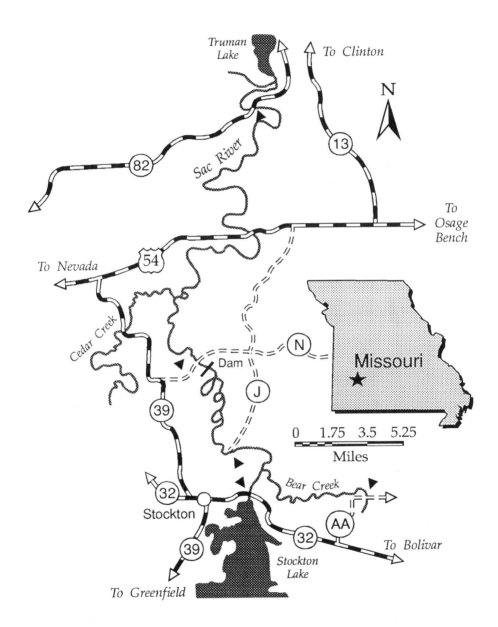

FLOAT 18 SAC RIVER

Region: Ozark Border
Difficulty: I, sometimes II
Quadrangles: Bearcreek, Bona, Aldrich, Caplinger Mills, Filley, Roscoe Stockton, Vista, Osceola
County Maps: Cedar, Polk, St. Clair
Statistics: Drainage: 1,970 sq. miles; Permanent Flow: 106 miles
Put in: Caplinger Mills access at the dam and bridge off County Road N
Take out: Vilhauer bridge access 8.3 miles on County Road W

The Float: The Sac River no longer flows free to the Osage River. It's interrupted by two very popular impoundments—Lake Stockon and Truman Lake. You'll find some excellent fishing in the section between these two lakes.

Two of the most popular fish in Missouri are the bass and catfish. You'll find plenty of these in the Sac River. But don't miss out on the walleye. It's a favorite fish in the upper Midwest, and it's becoming increasingly popular in Missouri. The walleye is prevalent in Stockton (in fact, many anglers travel from Minnesota and Wisconsin to fish here in March when their lakes remain frozen) and in Truman. The Truman population makes a run up the Sac to spawn in the early spring. You can find these fish around the Caplinger Mills area.

The Sac is a slow, shallow river between the dams. Power generation above Truman has changed the complexion of this stream. But it remains a good float. You see plenty of Ozark hardwood forests and limestone bluffs.

There are also two floatable tributaries to the Sac—Bear Creek just east Stockton and Cedar Creek northwest of Stockton.

For a long one-day fishing trip, put it at the Caplinger Mills access at the dam and bridge off County Road N and float to the Vilhauer bridge access 8.3 miles on County Road W. This area offers good walleye fishing in the early spring.

You can make this an excellent two-day run by continuing on seven miles to the Highway 54 bridge.

For short floats, try the tributaries. Put-in on Bear Creek at the County Road A bridge. It's a 7.2-mile run to the County Road M bridge.

For a longer run, it's an 18-mile run to the Sac River on Cedar Creek from the County Road K bridge.

According to an MDC survey of recreational value, the Sac River ranks 23rd of thirty-eight rivers and streams.

FLOAT 19 LOUTRE RIVER

Region: Ozark Border
Difficulty: I
Quadrangles: Pinnacle Lake, Americus, Hermann
County Maps: Montgomery
Statistics: Drainage 390 sq. miles; Permanent Flow thirty-two miles
Put in: County Road K bridge a .5 mile west of Big Spring
Take out: Highway 94 bridge at McKittrick

FLOAT 19 LOUTRE RIVER

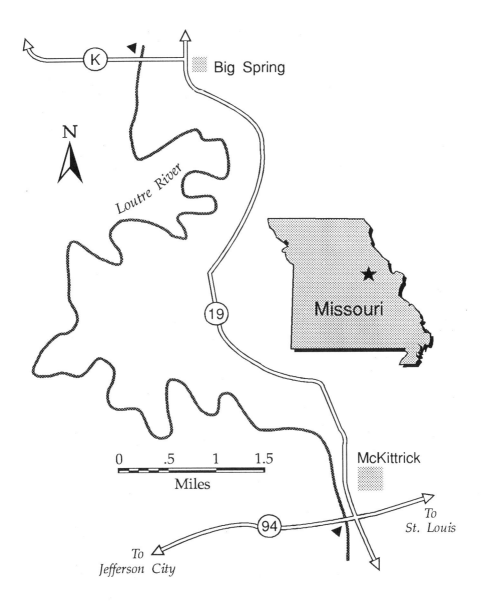

The float: Like most streams outside the Ozarks, there are no services or developed access areas on the Loutre River. While it's a gentle stream winding its way through rolling farmland, it requires an adventuresome spirit. The stretch from Big Spring to McKittrick is fourteen miles.

The Loutre flows slowly except during periods of high water. So fourteen miles is quite a paddle for a one-day trip. There are few suitable places to camp on the privately owned banks.

The area is thick with sycamores. You're likely to see many animals and birds that frequent bottomland, including deer, turkey, beaver, and squirrels.

Put in at the County Road K bridge a .5 mile west of Big Spring. The banks are steep. You may need ropes to lower the canoes. And don't forget your rubber boots. Take out at the Highway 94 bridge at McKittrick. The Missouri River is about four miles farther downstream.

FLOAT 20 BEAVER CREEK

Region: Ozarks
Difficulty: I and II
Quadrangles: Bradleyville, Forsyth, Protem
County Maps: Douglas, Taney
Statistics: Drainage Area: 402 sq. miles; Permanent Flow: 42.5 miles
Put in: Highway 76/125 bridge at Bradleyville
Take out: Highway 6 bridge east of Taneyville
Area outfitters:
• Beaver Canoe Rentals and Campgrounds Brownbranch, MO 65608, 417-796-2336 or 2406

The Float: Beaver Creek is another of the small Ozark streams that once fed the White River. Now it flows into Bull Shoals Lake through the Ozark hills. You'll see small farms, bluffs and mature hardwood forests.

Like several of the small creeks that fed the White River, Beaver Creek does not have a steady annual flow. In high water, you can float about forty miles from the headwaters near Jackson Mill to the spot where the water backs up into Bull Shoals.

In summer, Beaver Creek caters to anglers who like to wade and fish. Those who strictly want to float should begin at the Highway 76/125 bridge at Bradleyville and float 4.5 miles to the Highway 6 bridge east of Taneyville.

Above this run, from the Highway 76 bridge near Jackson Mill to Bradleyville, you'll find twenty-two miles of holes and shallow riffles in summer. The fishing is good, but you'll have to drag your canoe over the shallow riffles.

FLOAT 20 BEAVER CREEK

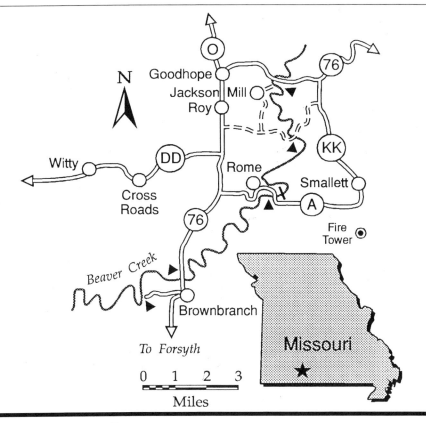

FLOAT 21 BIG PINEY RIVER

Region: Ozarks
Difficulty: I and II
Quadrangles: Bado, Big Piney, Edgar Springs, Houston, Prescott, Waynesville
County Maps: Phelps, Pulaski, Texas
Statistics: Drainage: 768 sq. miles; Permanent Flow: 96.5 miles
Put in: MDC Baptist Camp Access on County Road RA off Highway 63 or Tone Hogan Ford off County Road AU 3.5 river miles downstream
Take out: MDC Dog's Bluff Access 8.7 miles downstream at Highway 17.
For more information: National Forest Service headquarters in Rolla 314-364-4621.
Area outfitters:
- Boiling Spring Resort, Rt. 7, Box 124, Licking, MO 65542, 314-674-3488 or 2762;
- Ray's Riverside Resort, Rt. 7, Box 418, Licking, MO 65542, 314-674-2430;
- Rich's Last Resort, Rt. 1, Box 115, Duke, MO 65461, 314-435-6669;
- Wilderness Ridge Resort, Big Piney Route, Duke, MO 65461, 314-435-6767;

FLOAT 21 *BIG PINEY*

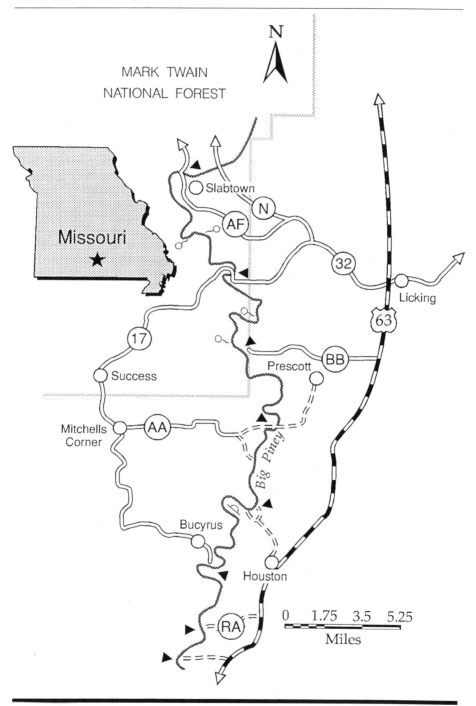

- Houston Canoe Rental, Houston Texaco 805 S., Sam Houston Blvd., Houston, MO 65483, 417-967-2488 or 9969

The float: The Big Piney ranks high in recreational value, according to an MDC survey. It's mean recreational value is a solid 7.5 out of ten, and it ranks seventh out of thirty-eight popular rivers and streams.

But the Big Piney is not without it's problems. Survey respondents ranked pollution as the number one problem here. Other problems include intensive agricultural use, heavy recreational use, sand and gravel dredging and shoreline development.

Despite these assaults, the Big Piney remains one of Missouri's better floats, especially in the upper reaches where you still see some pristine Ozark landscape—tall bluffs, evergreens and hardwoods, cool springs, deer and turkey.

You can launch a major expedition on the Big Piney, traveling eighty-five miles to the Gasconade River. From there, the Gasconade flows on to the Missouri River.

The fishing is good on the Big Piney for native smallmouth bass.

Begin your float at the MDC Baptist Camp Access on County Road RA off Highway 63. There is another access at Tone Hogan Ford off County Road AU 3.5 river miles downstream. For a day-trip, take out at the MDC Dog's Bluff Access 8.7 miles downstream at Highway 17.

For a multi-day float, begin your trip within the Mark Twain National Forest. You can camp free on these public lands, but be sure to get a map from the Forest Service. There are large tracts of private land within the National forest.

Put in at the MDC access at Boiling Spring on County Road BB. Your trip through the National Forest will take you past many springs, bluffs and Ozark hardwood forests. The MDC Mason Bridge Access is six miles from Boiling Spring—another good starting point off High way 32. Continue on to the MDC Ross Access twenty-nine miles from Boiling Spring. Do not float farther than Ross take-out. This is the last take-out before the Fort Leonard Wood Military Reservation.

FLOAT 22 BLACK RIVER

Region: Ozarks
Difficulty: I and II
Quadrangles: Edgehill, Ellington, Lesterville, Piedmont, Poplar Bluff, Williamsville
County Maps: Butler, Reynolds, Wayne
Statistics: Drainage Area: 2,686 sq. miles; Permanent Flow: 363 miles
For more information: about Johnson Shut-ins State Park, call 314-546-2450.
Put in: Iron Bridge or gravel road south of Lesterville
Take out: County Road K bridge
Area outfitters:
- Black River Floats and Canoe Rental, P.O. Box 1, Lesterville, MO 63654, 314-637-2247;
- Clearwater Store's, Rt. 3, Box 3592, Piedmont, MO 63957, 314-223-4813;
- Franklin Floats, Rt. 1, Box 9, Lesterville, MO 63654 314-637-2205;

FLOAT 22 BLACK RIVER

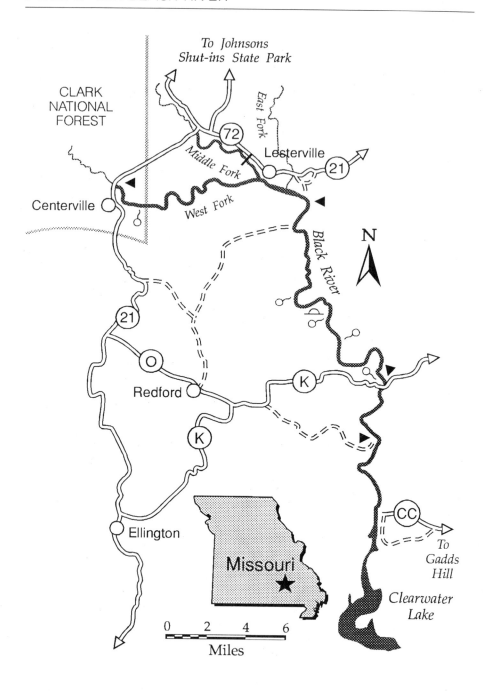

- Jeff's Canoe Rental, Star Route, Box 204-A, Annapolis, MO 63620, 314-598-4555;
- Keener Springs Recreation Area, Rt. 1, Box 188, Williamsville, MO 63967, 314-998-2837;
- Kemper's Hide-a-way, Rt. 3, Box 3641, Piedmont, MO 63957 314-223-7324;
- K-Mark Canoe Rental, Box 186, Annapolis, MO 63620, 314-598-3399;
- Markham Spring Canoe Rental, Rt. 1, Mill Spring, MO 63952;
- Parks Bluff Campground, P.O. Box 24, Lesterville, MO 63654, 314-637-2290;
- Secluded Trail, P.O. Box 48, Lesterville, MO 63654, 314-637-2245;
- Twin Rivers Landing, P.O. Box 150, Lesterville, MO 63654, 314-637-2274 or 800-331-6439;
- Wilderness Lodge, Peola Rd, Lesterville, MO 63654, 314-637-2295

The Float: The Black River tumbles out of the highest section of the Ozarks into the Mississippi lowlands. In between, you'll find some excellent floating and good fishing for smallmouth bass.

An MDC survey of recreational value ranks the Black River fourteenth of thirty-eight popular rivers and streams. Clearwater Reservoir interrupts the Black River. The best floating is above the dam.

Put in at the Iron Bridge on the gravel road south of Lesterville. The next fifteen miles to the County Road K bridge runs through Ozark forest and farm country. You'll see several springs, bluffs and caves.

Past the K bridge, the water begins backing up into Clearwater Reservoir. You'll continue to find good fishing below this point.

Don't forget to visit Johnson Shut-ins State Park on the East Fork of the Black River. It's not floatable, as this area's gradient is better than seventy-feet-per-mile. But you'll see spectacular rock formations—some of the oldest exposed rock in the country.

FLOAT 23 BRYANT CREEK

Region: Ozarks
Difficulty: I and II
Quadrangles: Buckhart, Gainsville
County Maps: Douglas, Ozark
Statistics: Drainage Area 613 sq. miles; Permanent Flow 54.5 miles
Put in: Highway 14 bridge near Sweden or Rippee Wildlife Area off Highway 14
Take out: One-day trip - to the Bertha Ford low-water bridge. Longer trips - continue on to the MDC Sycamore Access at Highway 181, twenty-six miles from the put-in.
Area outfitters:
- Ho-Lo Campground and Canoe Rental, Sycamore, MO 65758, 417-261-2590;
- Hodgson Water Mill, Smith Canoe Rental, Star Route 1, Box 24, Sycamore, MO 65758, 417-261-2568;
- Twin Bridges Canoe Rental, HCR-64, Box 230, West Plains, MO 65775, 417-265-7507

The float: Bryant Creek offers another wild experience in the White River system. This is a small, clear, fast stream with lots of sharp turns and brushy obstructions. The gradient averages six feet-per-mile. Fishing is also good on the Bryant. Like most Ozark streams, concentrate your efforts in the deep holes and quiet pools.

Put in at the Highway 14 bridge near Sweden. There's also the MDC Rippee Wildlife Area of Highway 14 where you can launch.

For a one-day trip, float about ten miles to the Bertha Ford low-water bridge. For longer trips, continue on to the MDC Sycamore Access at Highway 181, twenty-six miles from the put-in.

For the best runs, float in wet seasons. In summer, many rifles are too shallow to float a canoe—but these areas make wonderful places to wade and fish.

FLOAT 23 BRYANT CREEK

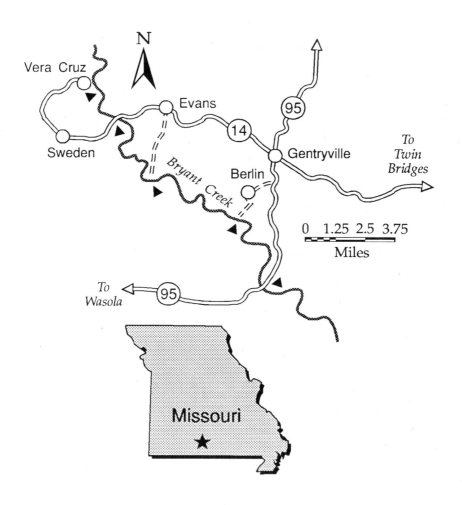

FLOAT 24 BULL CREEK

Region: Ozarks
Difficulty: I and II
Quadrangles: Branson, Day
County Maps: Christian, Taney
Statistics: Drainage Area: 206 sq. miles; Permanent Flow: twenty-three miles
Put in: low-water bridge on the gravel road off Highway 176 between Day and Walnut Shade
Take out: County Road F bridge

The float: Bull Creek is clear, small and fast with a gradient of ten feet per mile. You'll find some good fishing here for bass.

Begin your trip at the low-water bridge on the gravel road off Highway 176 between Day and Walnut Shade. There is a small falls at about five miles which you can run in high water, or bypass. Inspect this run first.

Take out at the County Road F bridge. Below this point is Lake Taneycomo. You'll find more good bass fishing in this slower water. Consider a multi-day trip that includes Lake Taneycomo where anglers catch stringers of large rainbow and brown trout.

FLOAT 25 SWAN CREEK

Region: Ozarks
Difficulty: I to III
Quadrangles: Forsyth, Garrison
County Maps: Christian, Taney
Statistics: Drainage Area: 192 sq. miles; Permanent Flow: thirty miles
Put in: Highway 125 bridge in Garrison
Take out: County Road AA bridge

The float: Swan Creek has a split personality. In the summer, when the weather is dry, the creek is a series of pools followed by riffles so shallow that a canoe won't float across most of them. It's a nice run for anglers who like to wade and fish the holes.

In wet seasons, particularly spring, the Swan rises quickly to form one of the best whitewater runs in the state with rapids rating Class III. The average gradient is ten-feet-per-mile.

Begin your trip at the Highway 125 bridge in Garrison. Take out seven miles downstream at the County Road AA bridge. For a whitewater run when the water is high, begin at the County Road AA bridge and canoe seven miles to the low-water bridge off the gravel road near Dickens. The area below this run gets wild in high water. It's another seven miles from here to the Highway 160 bridge.

In low water, this is a good run for beginners who like to fish the clear, rocky streams of the Ozarks. In high water, this stream is only for experienced intermediate and expert canoeists.

FLOAT 24 *BULL CREEK*
FLOAT 25 *SWAN CREEK*

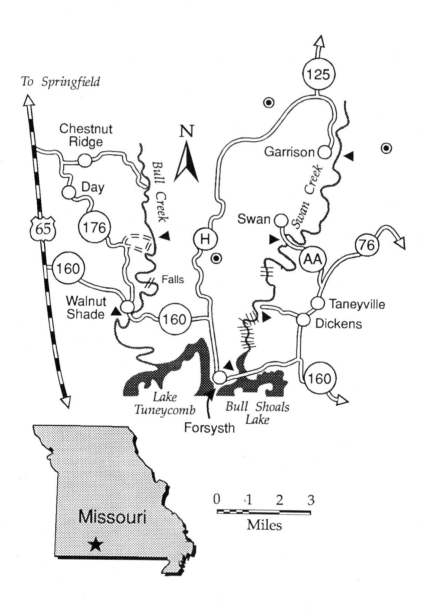

FLOAT 26 *COURTOIS CREEK*

Region: Ozarks
Difficulty: II
Quadrangles: Berryman, Sullivan
County Maps: Crawford, Washington
Statistics: Drainage 230 sq. miles; Permanent Flow 29.5 miles
For more information: Call the Forest Service Headquarters in Rolla at 314-364-4621.
Put in: The low-water bridge just east of Brazil. For a shorter trip, the low-water bridge on the gravel road off Highway 8 near the Courtois Creek Roadside Park.
Take out: MDC campground in the Huzzah Wildlife Area. 20.4 river miles downstream of Brazil and nine river miles downstream from the Courtois Creek Roadside Park.
Area outfitters: (also see Meramec River)
- Bass Canoe and Raft Rental, P.O. Box BB, Steelville, MO 65565, 800-392-3700;
- Courtois Canoe Rental, P.O. Box 122, Steelville, MO 65565, 314-786-7452;
- Huzzah Valley Stables, Campground and Canoe Rental, HC-87, Box 7480, Steelville, MO 65565, 800-392-0252 or 800-367-4516;
- Kevin's Canoe & Raft Rental, Rt. 2, Box 142-A, Cuba, MO 65453, 314-885-2947;
- Keyes Canoe & Raft Rental, Rt. 1, Box 120, Leasburg, MO 65535, 800-888-0023;
- Misty Valley Canoe Rental, HC-87, Box 7576, Steelville, MO 65565, 314-786-8151;
- The Rafting Company, P.O. Box 906, Steelville, MO 65565, 800-426-7238;

The float: Courtois is the twin of the Huzzah. They flow roughly parallel through a largely unspoiled Ozark landscape. Like the Huzzah, the Courtois is clear, shallow and cool.

Because it's not a major watershed, the Courtois wasn't included in the MDC survey of recreational value. If it had it would have ranked high. Canoeists enjoy the swiftness of the stream during periods of high water. Anglers enjoy wading and fishing the quiet pools when the water is low.

Both the Courtois and Huzzah are excellent streams for catching smallmouth bass. Look for them in the quiet, deep pools near cover such as rocks and fallen logs.

The length of the Courtois makes it perfect for a two-day adventure. The creek flows through the Mark Twain National Forest for most of its length. You may camp on these public lands, but be sure to get maps from the Forest Service because there are many tracks of private land within the National Forest. Begin at the low-water bridge just east of Brazil.

For a shorter trip, put in at the low-water bridge on the gravel road off Highway 8 near the Courtois Creek Roadside Park.

Take out at the MDC campground in the Huzzah Wildlife Area 20.4 river miles downstream of Brazil and nine river miles downstream from the Courtois Creek Roadside Park.

For the really adventuresome, continue to the confluence of the Meramec River and follow it twenty-two miles to Meramec State Park—a nice five-day trip overall.

FLOAT 26 *COURTOIS CREEK*
FLOAT 27 *HUZZAH CREEK*

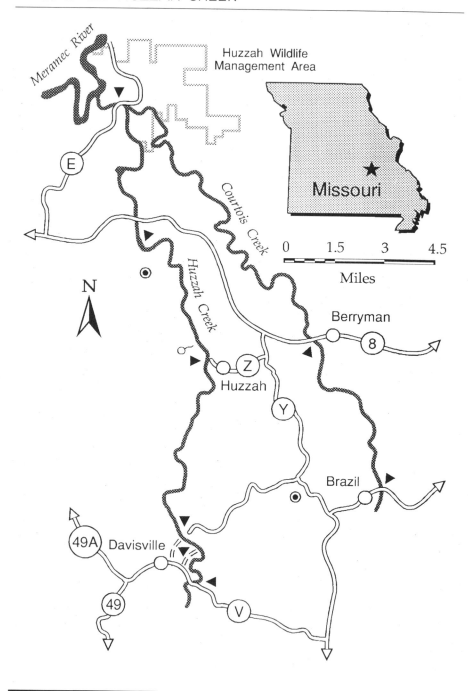

FLOAT 27 *HUZZAH CREEK*

Region: Ozarks
Difficulty: II
Quadrangles: Berryman, Sullivan
County Maps: Crawford, Washington
Statistics: Drainage 496 sq. miles; Permanent Flow thirty-three miles
For more information: Forest Service headquarters in Rolla 314-364-4621.
Put in: Begin at the County Road V bridge southeast of Davisville. For a shorter trip, the low-water bridge just northwest of the town of Huzzah.
Take out: MDC Scotia Bridge Access on County Road E 22.4 river miles from Davisville and twelve river miles from Huzzah
Area outfitters: See Courtois Creek

The float: Huzzah Creek is typical of the pristine Ozarks stream—clear, shallow and cool. It flows largely unspoiled toward its confluence with Courtois Creek and then on to the Meramec.

Because it's not a major watershed, the Huzzah wasn't included in the MDC survey of recreational value. If it had it would have ranked high. Canoeists enjoy the swiftness of the stream during periods of high water. Anglers enjoy wading and fishing the quiet pools when the water is low.

The length of the Huzzah makes it perfect for a two-day adventure. The creek flows through the Mark Twain National Forest for most of its length. You may camp on these public lands. But be sure to get maps from the Forest Service because there are many tracks of private land within the National Forest. Begin at the County Road V bridge southeast of Davisville.

For a shorter trip, put in at the low-water bridge just northwest of the town of Huzzah.

Take out at the MDC Scotia Bridge Access on County Road E 22.4 river miles from Davisville and twelve river miles from Huzzah.

FLOAT 28 *CURRENT RIVER*

Region: Ozarks
Difficulty: I and II
Quadrangles: Cedargrove, Cardareva, Doniphan, Grandin, Eminence, Lewis Hollow, Montauk, Round Spring, Van Buren
County Maps: Carter, Dent, Ripley, Shannon
Statistics: Drainage Area: 2,120 sq. miles; Permanent Flow: 134 miles
Put in: Baptist Camp near the Montauk State Park
Take out: one-day trip, take out at Cedargrove on County Road ZZ
For more information about Montauk State Park, call 314-548-2201. For Ozark National Scenic Riverways, call 314-232-4236.
Area outfitters: Current River
• Akers Ferry Canoe Rental, HCR-81, Box 90, Salem, MO 65560, 314-858-3224 or 800-333-5628;

FLOAT 28 CURRENT RIVER

- Carr's Canoe Rental, HCR-1, Box 137, Eminence, MO 65466 314-858-3240 (summer) 226-5459 (winter);
- Doniphan Canoe & Tube Rental, 204 W. Jefferson Doniphan, MO 63935, 314-996-7171;
- Hawthorne Canoe Rental, P.O. Box 615, Van Buren, MO 63965, 314-323-4274;
- Jadwin Canoe Rental and Campground, Rt. 1, Box 36 Jadwin, MO 65501, 314-729-5229;
- Neil Canoe and Jon Boat Rental P.O. Box 396, Van Buren, MO 63965, 314-323-4447 (summer) or 4356 (winter);
- Ozark Hills Canoe Rental and Campground, Rt. 1, Box 36 Jadwin, MO 65501, 314-729-7340;

- Round Spring Canoe Rental HCR-62, Box 360, Salem, MO 65560, 314-858-3237 or 800-365-2537;
- Running River Canoe Rental, HCR-62, Box 368, Salem, MO 65560 314-858-3371;
- Silver Arrow Canoe Rental, HCR-62, Box 164 Salem, MO 65560, 314-729-5770 or 800-333-6040;
- Wild River Canoe Rental, HCR-62, Box 260, Salem, MO 65560; 314-858-3230 or 800-333-5628.

Current River and Jacks Fork River
- Adventure Kayaks & Canoes, P.O. Box 276, Eminence, MO 65466, 314-226-3642;
- Alley Spring Canoe Rental, Alley Spring, MO 65466, 314-226-3386;
- Big Spring Canoe & Tube Rental, Hwy. 60, Van Buren, MO 63965, 314-323-4550 or 4168 (nights);
- Current River Canoe Rental, HCR-62, Box 375, Salem, MO 65560, 314-858-3250 or 226-5517;
- Eminence Canoe, Cottages and Campground, Box 276, Eminence, MO 65466, 314-226-3642;
- Leuckel's Landing, 1 Big Spring Rd., Van Buren, MO 63965, 314-323-8433;
- Scenic Rivers Canoe Rental, P.O. Box 581 Eminence, MO 65466, 314-226-3386;
- Two Rivers Canoe Rental HCR-2, Box 199, Eminence, MO 65466, 314-226-3478;
- Windy's Canoe Rental, Box 151, Eminence, MO 65466, 314-226-3404

The float: There are few experienced floaters nationwide who have not heard of the Current River. It is one of two Missouri Rivers designated as an Ozark National Scenic Riverway. Along its winding path, you'll find some of the best fishing and most unspoiled Ozark scenery anywhere in the state.

Almost the entire length of the Current in Missouri is protected either by the National Park Service or the National Forest Service (Mark Twain National Forest).

The Current is a gentle stream with very little Class II water and an average gradient of five-feet-per-mile.

An MDC survey ranks the Current River first of thirty-eight popular rivers and streams for recreational value. And it is this top ranking that most adversely affects the river. According to the survey: "The Current River may be a classic example of a stream which is being loved to death. Even if the current and future problems of the watershed can be overcome, this resource is expected to lose its top ranking...This loss may be due to an expected increase in the recreational use of many of the major streams located near metropolitan areas. It may also indicate a pessimistic attitude toward the control of the problems associated with intensive recreational use."

In other words, during the peak summer season, the Current is crowded with canoes, kayaks, float tubes, and, farther down river, jet skis, johnboats and other watercraft.

The Current is a big river. Below Big Spring, you'll find a lot of motor boats. But the areas above offer excellent floating—especially the fifteen miles between Baptist Camp Access and Akers Ferry. Because the Current is the most spring-fed of Missouri's rivers, you can float year-round.

Put in at Baptist Camp near the Montauk State Park. This section to

You'll find plenty of developed and undeveloped camping along streams flowing through the Mark Twain National Forest and along National Scenic Rivers like the Current—Missouri's most popular floating and fishing stream. Missouri Division of Tourism Photo.

Cedargrove is the MDC trophy trout management area. Fishing is excellent for large rainbows.

For a one-day trip, take out at Cedargrove on County Road ZZ. Or use the campground here for a base camp for a two-day float. Continue on to Akers Ferry. The three miles above Akers offers excellent fishing for trout and smallmouth. Cast jigs, crankbaits and spinners to the submerged rocks.

The Current River flows through Montauk State Park, one of Missouri's four trout parks. The park offers camping, cabins, and trout fishing for a $2 daily tag. It's also a good place to spot bald eagles that spend the winter in this area.

FLOAT 29 *ELEVEN POINT RIVER*

Region: Ozarks
Difficulty: I and II
Quadrangles: Birch Tree, Gatewood, Montier, Van Buren
County Maps: Oregon
Statistics: Drainage Area 1,000 sq miles; Permanent Flow fifty miles
Put in: gravel road off Highway 19 near Greer
Take out: Turner's Mill near Surprise
Area outfitters:
• Hufstedler's Store & Canoe Rental Riverton Rural Branch, Alton, MO 65606, 417-778-6116;

- Richard's Canoe Rental, Rt. 2, Alton, MO 65606, 417-778-6186;
- Wood's Float and Canoe Rental, Rt. 2, Box 2549, Alton, MO 65606, 417-778-6497 or 6144

The float: The Eleven Point River flows through a wild section of the Mark Twain National Forest. Here you'll find mature forests, limestone bluffs and numerous springs, including the famous Greer Spring. Although Greer Spring is privately owned, the owners allow the public to hike around it. They've left the spring in a natural state making it one of the best preserved in Missouri.

The Eleven Point is a gentle stream and has an average gradient of five-feet-per-mile. You can float the middle section, described below, year round. The upper river may not always be floatable in dry weather. Check water levels before you travel.

An MDC survey ranks the Eleven Point third in recreational value of thirty-eight popular rivers and streams. Like the Current and Jacks Fork, the over-riding concern is intense recreational use.

Put in at Cane Bluff on the gravel road off Highway 19 near Greer. Float the twelve-mile section between here and Turner's Mill near Surprise. Take two days and camp at the Highway 19 bridge. You'll find a trail here to the Greer Spring.

FLOAT 29 ELEVEN POINT RIVER

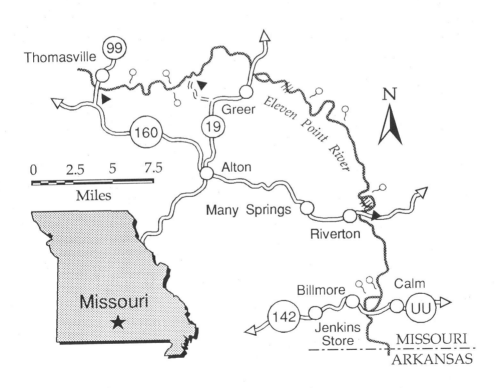

FLOAT 30 ELK RIVER/BIG SUGAR CREEK

Region: Ozarks
Difficulty: II
Quadrangles: Noel, Rocky Comfort
County Maps: MacDonald
Statistics: Drainage Area (to the state line) 850 sq. miles; Permanent Flow 21.5 miles
Put in: MDC Deep Ford Access
Take out: MDC Mt. Shira Access off Highway 59.
Area outfitters:
- Dube's Three River Campground, P.O. Box 697, Pineville, MO 64856, 417-223-4746;
- Elk River Floats and Campground, R.R. 1, Noel, MO 64854, 417-475-3561;
- Kozy Camp, Hwy. 71, Pineville, MO 64856, 417-223-4586 or 4832;
- Shady Beach, P.O. Box 473, Noel, MO 64854, 417-475-6483;
- Sycamore Landing Drawer H, Noel, MO 64854, 417-475-6460

The float: The Elk River, along with its major tributary the Big Sugar Creek, is a lively Class II river with an average gradient of 6.6-feet-per-mile. It is suitable for intermediate canoeists and beginners who have made a few successful runs on some of Missouri's more placid streams.

While the Elk flows through some rugged country in southwestern Missouri, it is crowded with floaters and cottage development in some areas. An MDC survey gave the Elk/Big Sugar a 6.9 score out of ten for recreational value. Overall, the river ranked twenty-fourth of thirty-eight popular rivers and streams. The survey shows this rank will drop in the coming years due mostly to intensive recreational use.

Its proximity to Spring field and Joplin accounts for a great deal of the river's popularity. The Elk/Big Sugar is a clear stream and offers excellent fishing.

An interesting twelve-mile run that takes you through some wild and developed sections of the Elk begins at the MDC Deep Ford Access on the gravel road northeast of Pineville. There is a low-water bridge just before the MDC area that makes a good access.

Less than four miles downstream, the Little Sugar Creek (see Little Sugar/Indian Creek) joins the Big Sugar forming the Elk River. Take out at the MDC MT. Shira Access off Highway 59.

For longer runs in wilder country, begin farther up the Big Sugar Creek at Powell where you'll find access at two bridges near town. Take out at the low-water bridge in Cyclone or continue on to the Deep Ford Access for a two-day trip.

FLOAT 30 ELK RIVER/BIG SUGAR CREEK

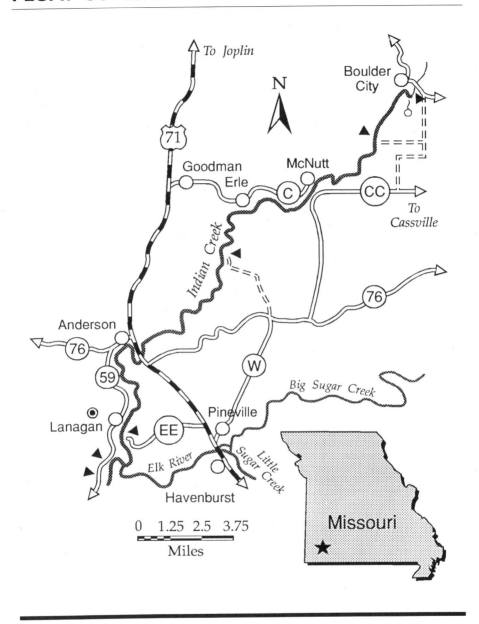

Floating gets crowded in the summer on the popular streams in the Ozarks. Missouri Division of Tourism Photo.

FLOAT 31 *FLAT CREEK*

Region: Flat Creek/OZ
River: Flat Creek
Difficulty: I and II
Quadrangles: Aurora, Shell Knob
County Maps: Barry, Stone
Statistics: Drainage Area: 314 sq. miles; Permanent Flow: 49.5 miles
Put in: multiple-day trip, put in at the MDC Stubblefield Access off Highway 248 near Jenkins
Take out: Highway 173 bridge north of Cape Fair

FLOAT 31 *FLAT CREEK*

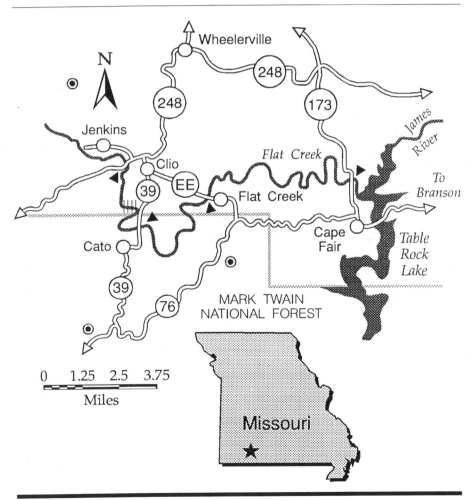

Area outfitters:
• Fletcher's Devil's Dive Resort, HCR-1, Box 8, Eagle Rock, MO 65641, 417-271-3396

The float: Flat Creek is part of the White River system. It now flows into Table Rock Lake. It is a good fishing stream for smallmouth ass and offers a quick twenty-six-mile run with a gradient of seven-feet-per-mile.

For a multiple-day trip, put in at the MDC Stubblefield Access off Highway 248 near Jenkins. Make your first day's run to the MDC Lower Flat Creek Access fourteen miles downstream. This is a good place to camp, or a good alternate put-in for a run down the lower river. Continue on to the Highway 173 bridge north of Cape Fair.

FLOAT 32 GASCONADE RIVER

Region: Ozarks
Difficulty: I
Quadrangles: Bland, Drynob, Linn, Mansfield N.E. Manes, Owens, Morrison, Richland, Rolla, Vienna, Waynesville
County Maps: Gasconade, Laclede, Maries, Osage, Phelps, Pulaski, Wright
Statistics: Drainage Area 3,600 sq. miles; Permanent Flow 263 miles
Put in: Forest Service access on the gravel road south of Falcon
Take out: MDC Hazelgreen Access at the Interstate 44 bridge
For more information Mark Twain National Forest, headquarters in Rolla, 314-364-4621
Area outfitters:
• Fredericksburg Ferry Canoe & Boat Rental, R.R. 1, Box 212, Morrison, MO 65061, 314-294-7203;
• Hilkemeyer's Boat & Canoe Rental, Hwy. 63 South, Freeburg, MO 65035, 314-744-5245;
• Indian Forest Resort, Hwy. 42 East, Vienna, MO 65582, 314-422-3484;
• Ozark Springs Resort, HCR-75, Box 220, Richland, MO 65556, 314-765-5223;
• Gasconade Valley Campground and Canoe Rental, P.O. Box 100, Jerome, MO 65529, 314-762-2526;
• Shafer Canoe Rental, Box 22, Linn, MO 65051, 314-897-3662;
• Gasconade Hills, HCR-73, Box 170, Richland, MO 65556, 314-765-3044 or 800-869-6861 (reservations);

The float: The Gasconade is the longest river confined to Missouri. It is also the most crooked and offers the most floating opportunities.

An MDC survey of recreational value ranks the Gasconade fourth of thirty-eight popular rivers and streams. No wonder. There are dozens of access points, calm water and a variety of fish and wildlife. The problems on the Gasconade include intense agricultural and recreational use as well as poor land use. But survey respondents say these problems are only moderate. The Gasconade, which was once considered for National Scenic Riverway status, will continue to be one of the most popular of all Missouri rivers.

For the true adventurer, the trip from the Highway 38 bridge near Hartville to the Missouri River covers 253 miles—between eighteen to thirty days. Along

FLOAT 32 *GASCONADE RIVER, MIDDLE*

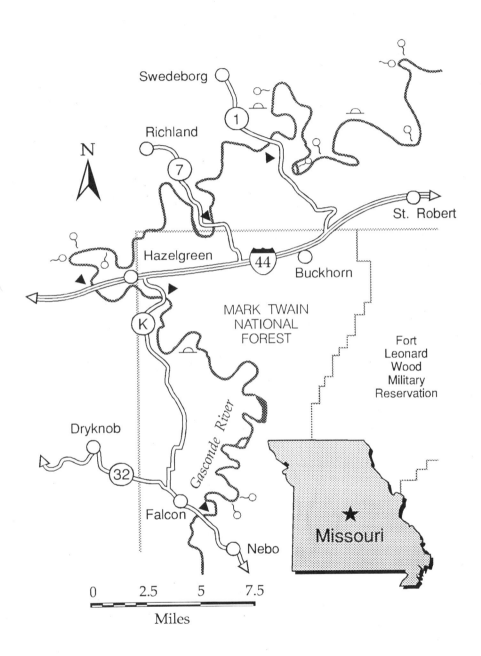

GASCONADE RIVER, LOWER

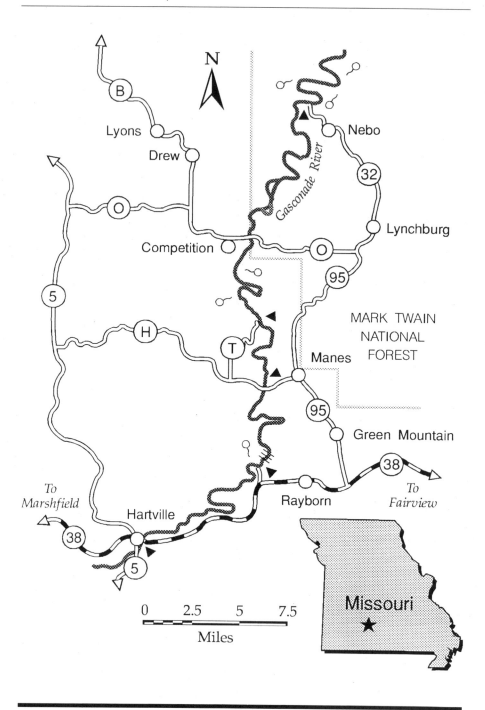

the route you'll find plenty of services, campgrounds, towns and even a fair amount of wilderness.

For shorter trips, consider the area in the Mark Twain National Forest. Put in at the Forest Service access on the gravel road south of Falcon. This is an area of forest and springs that stretches thirty miles to the MDC Hazelgreen Access at the Interstate 44 bridge. You may camp along the route anywhere in the national forest. Be sure to get maps from the Forest Service because there is some private land within the federal areas.

FLOAT 33 INDIAN CREEK/LITTLE SUGAR CREEK

Region: Ozarks
Difficulty: II and III
Quadrangles: Neosho, Noel, Richey
County Maps: MacDonald
Statistics: Drainage Area 217 sq. miles; Permanent Flow twenty-six miles
Put in: Highway D. Bridge near Boulder City
Take out: County Road CC bridge near McNatt
Area outfitters:
• Indian Creek Canoes and Campground, Hwy. 71, Anderson, MO 64831, 417-845-6400

The float: An excellent, fast spring run for intermediate canoeists is Indian Creek, a major tributary of the Elk River. The gradient is a nearly steady 8.6-feet-per-mile. Unlike the Elk River, there is little development here.

Put in at the Hwy. D bridge near Boulder City. Make a seven-mile run to the County Road CC bridge near McNatt. Portage around the dam at McNatt.

Another good run begins at McNatt and flows thirteen miles to the MDC Town Hole Access. This also makes a good put-in for a trip down the Elk River.

Little Sugar Creek is another, smaller tributary of the Elk River. Use it for an alternate start for an Elk River trip. Put in at the Hwy. 90 bridge near Jane. It's an eight-mile run to the Elk River.

FLOAT 34 JACKS FORK RIVER

Region: Ozarks
Difficulty: I and II
Quadrangles: Eminence, Summersville
County Maps: Shannon, Texas
Statistics: Drainage Area: 422 sq. miles; Permanent Flow: thirty-nine miles
Put in: MDC South Prong Access at the County Road Y bridge
Take out: Eminence or for a shorter trip, Salvation Army Camp nine miles downstream off Highway 17
For more information: about the Ozark National Scenic Riverways, 314-232-4236.
Area outfitters: See Current River;
• Jacks Fork Canoe Rental, P.O. Box 188, Eminence, MO 65466, 314-226-3434 or 800-333-5628

FLOAT 33 *INDIAN CREEK/LITTLE SUGAR CREEK*

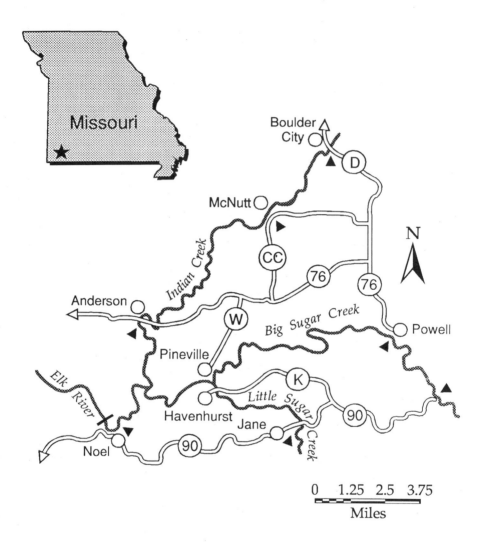

The float: The Jacks Fork is another of the Ozark National Scenic Riverways administered by the National Park Service—protected over most of its length to its confluence with the Current River.

An MDC survey ranks the Jacks Fork fifth in recreational value out of thirty-eight popular rivers and streams. Like the Current, the MDC expects this ranking to fall. According to the survey: "The slippage...parallels the fate of the Current. In both cases, future intensive recreational use is perceived to be the principal factor." The survey further indicates that most respondents believe nothing can be done about the problem of too many people wanting to enjoy the Jacks Fork River. And there's a lot to enjoy.

Unlike most Missouri streams, you can travel for miles without ever seeing a farm. Much of the Jacks Fork is a canyon. You'll also see mature hardwood forests, bluffs and caves.

The Jacks Fork is a gentle stream with a less reliable water flow than the Current. The average gradient is seven-feet-per-mile. You can float most of its length in the spring. But in summer, be sure to check the water levels before you travel.

Put in at the MDC South Prong Access at the County Road Y bridge. The thirty-eight miles between here and Eminence makes an excellent three- or four-day trip. Be sure to camp well above the river if there's any chance of rain. For a shorter trip, take out at the Salvation Army Camp nine miles downstream off Highway 17.

FLOAT 34 *JACKS FORK RIVER*

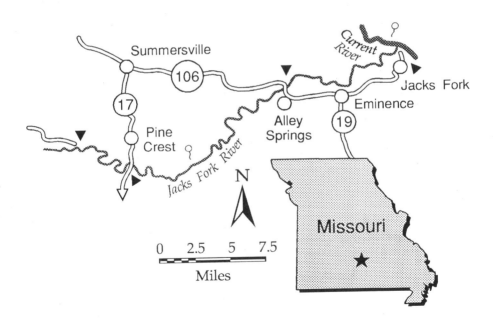

Be sure to check water levels with your outfitter or the Missouri Department of Conservation before floating. In summer, some streams become quite low. Missouri Division of Tourism.

FLOAT 35 *JAMES RIVER/FINLEY RIVER*

Region: Ozarks
Difficulty: I
Quadrangles: Galena, Highlandville, Hurley, Nixa, Ozark, Republic
County Maps: Christian, Green, Stone
Statistics: Drainage Area: 1,460 sq. miles; Permanent Flow: eighty-five miles
Put in: MDC Delaware Town Access off of Highway 14 west of Nixa
Take out: MDC Shelvin Rock Access off the gravel road east of Boaz

The float: The James River flows into Table Rock Lake which is one of the many impoundments on the White River system in Missouri and Arkansas. The White River is gone in Missouri and just a portion of its tributaries remain.

The James River and other tributaries of the White River remain popular for floating and fishing—especially because they are so close to Springfield and are easily accessible.

An MDC survey shows the James River ranks seventeenth of thirty-eight in recreational value among Missouri most popular rivers and streams. The survey suggests this rank will rise.

There are problems on the James. The two worst are pollution and intensive recreational use. According to the MDC survey: "The proximity of this stream to the City of Springfield is both a great recreational asset and a liability. Future pressures of human use from municipal and industrial water needs, sewage disposal and recreational uses suggests the potential for substantial conflicts..."

Toward the headwaters, the James offers a pleasant float for canoes, rafts, and tubes. The closer you get to Table Rock Lake, the more johnboats you'll see. The popular johnboat is twenty feet long and four feet wide. River fishermen developed these unique boats in the Ozarks for floating the White River system.

For a short fishing trip, begin at the MDC Delaware Town Access off of Highway 14 west of Nixa. Float to the MDC Shelvin Rock Access off the gravel road east of Boaz 6.5 miles downstream.

For strictly a canoe trip, put in at the Highway 125 bridge near Turner and float to the MDC Joe Crighton Access off County Road J seven miles downstream. For a longer run, continue on to Lake Springfield another 5.5 miles downstream.

There's a small tributary of the James River called the Finley River and you'll find some good smallmouth bass fishing here. From the Highway 125 bridge at Linden, it's a nineteen-mile trip to the James River. You'll find an access two-thirds of the way downstream at the dam and bridge above Highway 160.

FLOAT 35 *JAMES RIVER/FINLEY RIVER*

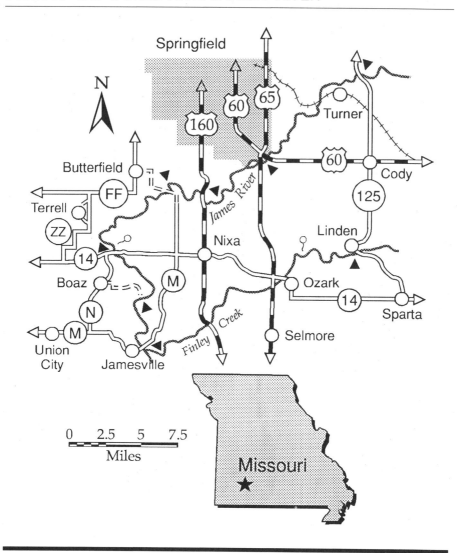

Fly fishermen reach some of Missouri's best fishing only by canoe. Tracker Marine Photo.

FLOAT 36 *MERAMEC RIVER*

Region: Ozarks
Difficulty: I
Quadrangles: Maramec Spring, Stone Hill, Steelville, Cuba, Leasburg, Sullivan, Union, St. Clair, Pacific, House Springs, Manchester, Eureka, Kirkwood, Maxville, Oakville
County Maps: Dent, Crawford, Franklin, Jefferson, St. Louis
Statistics: Drainage Area: 3,980 sq. miles; Permanent Flow: 201 miles
Put in: MDC Sappington Bridge Access on the gravel road off County Road D
Take out: Meramec Caverns and La Jolla Springs Access eleven miles downstream
For more information: Meramec State Park 314-468-6072. For cabin and canoe rental, call 314-468-6519; Onondaga Cave State Park, 314-245-6417.
Area outfitters: (also see Courtois Creek)
 • ABC Canoe Rental and Campground, P.O. Box 126 Cuba, MO 65453, 314-885-3222 or 775-5651 (weekends)
 • Adventure Floating and Camping, P.O. Box AM, Steelville, MO 65565, 314-775-5005
 • Arapaho Canoe Rentals and Campground, 351 Arapaho, Sullivan, MO 63080, 314-468-3218 or 6726

- Bird's Nest Lodge and Canoe Rental, P.O. Box 783, Steelville, MO 65565, 314-775-2606
- Blue Springs Campground and Canoe Rental, P.O. Box 540, Bourbon, MO 65441, 314-732-5200
- Cowboys Campground and Canoe Rental, Rt. 2, Box 2118, Cuba, MO 65453, 314-885-2841 or 800-448-1226
- Don's Bait & Tackle Boat & Canoe Rental, 1340 Parkway Dr., St. Clair, MO 63077, 314-629-1712 or 1834
- Fagan's Meramec River Canoe and Raft Rental, P.O. Box 796, Steelville, MO 65565, 314-775-5744
- Green's Meramec Canoe and Raft Rental, Rt. 1, Box 761, Steelville, MO 65565, 314-775-5595
- Jim's Landing and Floats, Inc., 1557 Grafs Landing Dr., St. Clair, MO 63077, 314-629-3284
- Onondaga Canoe Rental, Onondaga Cave State Park Hwy. H, Leasburg, MO 65535, 314-245-6600
- Ray's Canoe Rental, Rt. 1, Box 754, Steelville, MO 65565, 314-775-5697
- Saranac Springs Campground, Rt. 1, Box 230, Leasburg, MO 65535, 314-245-6620
- Uncle Lex's Raft and Canoe Rental, Hwy. W, Stanton, MO 63079, 314-927-5215

The float: The proximity of the Meramec River and its tributaries to St. Louis make it an important recreational river. It ranks very high in mean recreational value, according to the MDC recreational value survey, scoring 9.1 out of 10 points. The Meramec ranks third in recreational value among thirty-eight of Missouri's most popular rivers and streams.

Despite being close to a major city, the Meramec offers almost 200 miles of canoeing in a largely natural setting. Urban sites rule the river past St. Clair. Numerous springs feed the river making its waters clear and cool—a good place to fish for trout and smallmouth bass.

You'll see lots of caves and bluffs along the Meramec. Wildlife in the area includes deer, turkey, and bobcat.

For an excellent one-day float, put in at the MDC Sappington Bridge Access on the gravel road off County Road D. This float takes you through Meramec State Park.

Along the river near and in the park you'll see tall bluffs, cool springs, and several caves. In the park's interior you'll find even more springs and more than thirty caves. A particular favorite is Fisher Cave. The DNR leads tours through this cave known for its calcite deposits that form towering thirty-foot columns.

The Meramec Upland Forest Natural Area is the state's largest example of an undisturbed Ozark chert forest.

The park has modern services, including camping, a general store, and a dining lodge. The park also rents canoes making this a perfect base to float the river.

Take out at the Meramec Caverns and La Jolla Springs Access eleven miles downstream.

By camping in the park, you can extend your trip a few miles or float as far as the Mississippi. Continue on for two days to the County Road K bridge southeast of St. Clair. From here, it's eighty-one miles to the big river.

FLOAT 36 *MERAMEC RIVER*

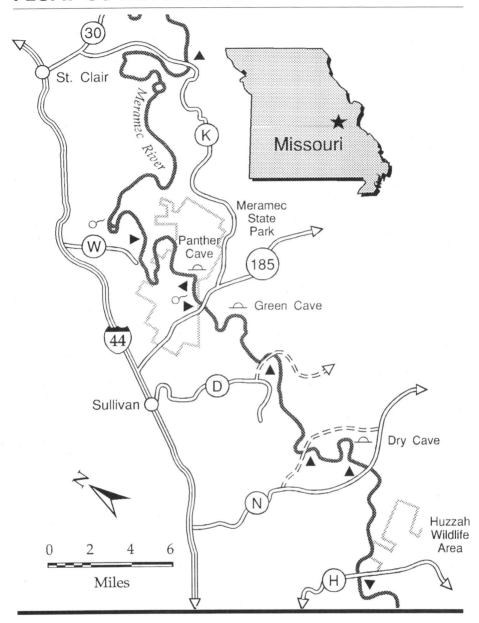

The Meramec also flows by the Onondaga Cave State Park. This isn't surprising. Missouri is also known as the cave state because we have more than 5,000. The Onondaga is one of the most dazzling in the country because of the quality of its formations.

The park offers a cave tour, camping, picnicking, hiking, swimming, dining, and canoe rental.

FLOAT 37 MOREAU RIVER

Region: Ozark Border
Difficulty: I
Quadrangles: Centertown, Eugene, Jefferson City, Meta
County Maps: Cole, Moniteau
Statistics: Drainage Area: 580 sq. miles; Permanent Flow: thirty-four miles
Put in: South Moreau Creek, the County Road AA bridge near Russellville. North Moreau Creek, Rockhouse Bridge just north of Russellville
Take out: South Moreau Creek, nine miles later at the low-water bridge on County Road D. North Moreau Creek, the low-water bridge at Murphy Ford about eight miles downstream. It's another sixteen miles to the junction with South Moreau Creek.

The float: The Moreau River flows northward to the Missouri River past the state capitol of Jefferson City. It's proximity to two small urban areas—the other is Columbia—makes it a popular stream, although it was not included in the MDC recreational value survey.

You'll find some excellent fishing here, including bass and catfish. A good one-day trip begins on the South Moreau Creek at the County Road AA bridge near Russellville. This route takes you through some good fishing territory. Take out nine miles later at the low-water bridge on County Road D.

On the North Moreau Creek, put in at Rockhouse Bridge just north of Russellville. For a day trip, take out at the low-water bridge at Murphy Ford about eight miles downstream. It's another sixteen miles to the junction with South Moreau Creek.

FLOAT 38 NIANGUA RIVER

Region: Ozarks
Difficulty: I and II
Quadrangles: Buffalo, Charity, Long Lane, Mack's Creek
County Maps: Camden, Dallas, Laclede
Statistics: Drainage Area: 1,040 sq. miles; Permanent Flow ninety-nine miles
Put in: Bennett Spring Access by the Highway 64 bridge
Take out: MDC Prosperine Access on the gravel road off County Route NN
For more information: Bennett Spring State Park, 417-532-4338.
Area outfitters:
- Can You Canoe, Rt. 16, Box 971, Lebanon, MO 65536, 417-532-6600
- Fort Bennett Canoe Rental, Route 16, Box 575, Lebanon, MO 65536, 417-588-1391
- Ho-Humm Canoe Rental and Campground, Rt. 16, Box 1206, Lebanon, MO 65536, 417-588-1908
- Maggard's Canoe and Corkery Campground, Rt. 3, Box 69, Lebanon, MO 65536, 417-532-7616
- Niangua River Oasis Canoe Rental, Rt. 16, Box 971, Lebanon, MO 65536, 417-532-6333 or 588-3797

FLOAT 37 *MOREAU RIVER*

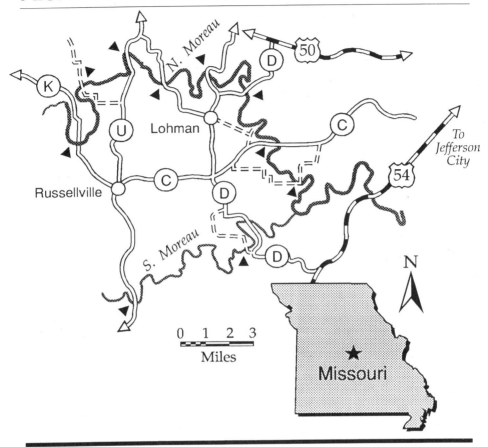

- Sand Spring Resort, Rt. 16, Box 1040, Lebanon, MO 65536, 417-532-5857
- R&W Canoe Rental & Campground, Rt. 16, Box 884, Lebanon, MO 65536, 417-588-3358
- Vogel's Canoe Rental, Rt. 16, Box 585, Lebanon, MO 65536, 417-532-4097

The float: When the MDC did its recreational value survey for popular Missouri rivers and streams, the Niangua River ranked 9th and had a mean recreational value of 8.1 out of 10. But the MDC expects those numbers to fall. According to the survey, the Niangua may fall from 9th to 19th.

The biggest reason is intensive recreational use—especially in the summer. There are many canoe outfitters catering to thousands of visitors annually. On a typical summer weekend, you'll see dozens of group floats banging their way along in aluminum canoes.

For some, this is part of the fun of floating—being with a large group of friends floating and partying the day away. More power to 'em. But this does detract from those seeking a natural experience or trying to fish.

And the Niangua offers both good fishing and a fine natural experience as

The Niangua River is one of the most popular in Missouri, noted for its easy paddling, clear water, excellent fishing and numerous springs. Tracker Marine Photo.

long as you float in the spring or fall. Summer is for the party crowd. If you like a party, you'll love the Niangua.

It is a gentle stream, but there are stretches of Class II water—and they sneak up on you. Be careful, especially in crowds. One mishap often sets up a chain reaction with other canoes. That's how crowded it can be.

The Niangua flows past one of the most popular parks in Missouri—Bennett Spring State Park. There's no floating allowed in the park, but it's a great place to camp. Bennett's major attraction is trout fishing. The hatchery there releases trout into the spring branch where anglers cast for their five-fish daily limit.

Other attractions at the park include the spring which pumps 100 million gallons of water per day into the Niangua and the nature center where a full-time naturalist offers lectures and nature walks.

Begin your float at the Bennett Spring Access by the Highway 64 bridge. This is an excellent wide access, but it may be crowded. If you like to fish for trout, drift worms and salmon eggs in the first few miles downstream. Also cast small jigs and crankbaits for smallmouth bass.

Take out at the MDC Prosperine Access on the gravel road off County Route NN.

In the spring, the Niangua is a perfect stream for a 2-day float. There are plenty of gravel bars for camping. Canoe outfitters in the area also offer multi-day canoeing packages. These packages are a great way for beginners to learn canoe camping.

The North Fork River is a popular destination in the Ozarks. Missouri Division of Tourism Photo.

FLOAT 38 NIANGUA RIVER

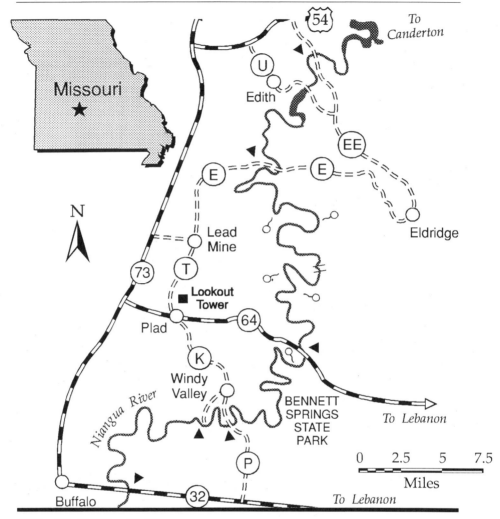

FLOAT 39 NORTH FORK OF THE WHITE RIVER

Region: Ozarks
Difficulty: I and II
Quadrangles: Cureall, Gainesville, Thornfield, Topaz
County Maps: Douglas, Ozark
Statistics: Drainage Area 1,310 sq. miles; Permanent Flow 189 miles
Put in: Highway 76 bridge north of Topaz
Take out: Hammond Camp Access a half mile upstream from Blue Springs
For more information: Forest Service headquarters in Rolla at 314-364-4621.
Area outfitters: (also see Bryant Creek);
• North Fork River Outfitters, Box 33, Dora, MO 65637, 417-261-2259 or 2345;

- River Side Canoe Rental, Caufield, MO 65626, 417-284-3043;
- Sunburst Ranch, HCR-68, Box 140, Caufield, MO 65626, 417-284-3443.

The float: The White River is gone. The North Fork is left to remind us of what the Ozarks once offered.

The North Fork River is spring-fed and has an ample year-round flow that makes for excellent floating and fishing. Despite its low difficulty rating, the North Fork offers some fine whitewater rides. The average gradient is 7.4-feet-per-mile.

The best float on the North Fork is that area within the Mark Twain National Forest. Federal protection insures that sections of this float will remain truly wild. You may camp anywhere along the river within the National Forest. Be sure to get Forest Service maps of the area as there is some private land within the forest.

Begin your trip at the Highway 76 bridge north of Topaz and float the thirty miles between here and Blue Spring. This makes an excellent three- to five-day trip using National Forest Service facilities. Take out at the Hammond Camp Access a half mile upstream from Blue Spring.

The North Fork rates eight out of ten for recreational value, according to an MDC survey. It ranks twelfth out of thirty-eight popular rivers and streams in Missouri. But the MDC survey shows this ranking will slide badly in the coming years due to intense recreational use and shoreline development. For any chance at a wild experience reminiscent of the old White River, stick to the section within the Mark Twain National Forest.

FLOAT 40 *OSAGE FORK OF THE GASCONADE*

Region: Ozarks
Difficulty: I and II
Quadrangles: Drynob, Lebannon, Rader
County Maps: Laclede, Webster
Statistics: Drainage Area 520 sq. miles, Permanent Flow 69.5 miles
Put in: MDC Rader Access off County Road ZZ
Take out: MDC Drynob Access at Highway 32
Area outfitters: See Gasconade River

The float: The Gasconade River gets all the attention. The Osage Fork, however, offers a wonderful float through Ozark farm country. You'll see plenty of springs, caves, bluffs, and forests. You'll find numerous gravel bars for camping (most of the land is private).

Begin your trip at the MDC Rader Access off County Road ZZ. It's almost a forty-mile run to the MDC Drynob Access at Highway 32. But you can shorten the trip at several bridges and low-water bridges along the route.

Be sure to take a fishing pole on this float. You'll want to cast for bass, sunfish and catfish in the deep holes.

FLOAT 39 NORTH FORK OF THE WHITE RIVER

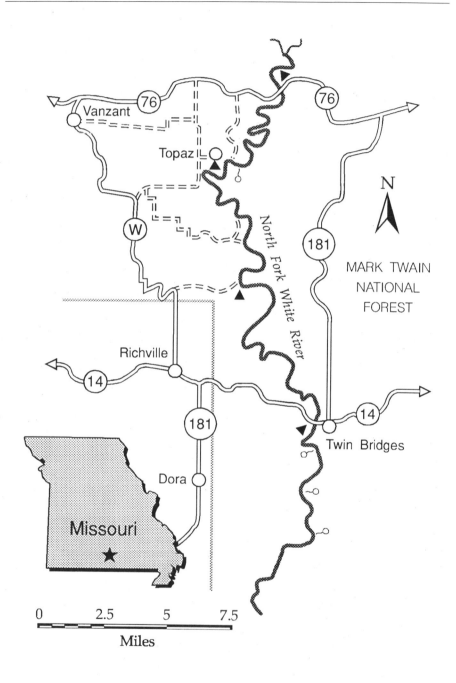

FLOAT 40 OSAGE FORK OF THE GASCONADE

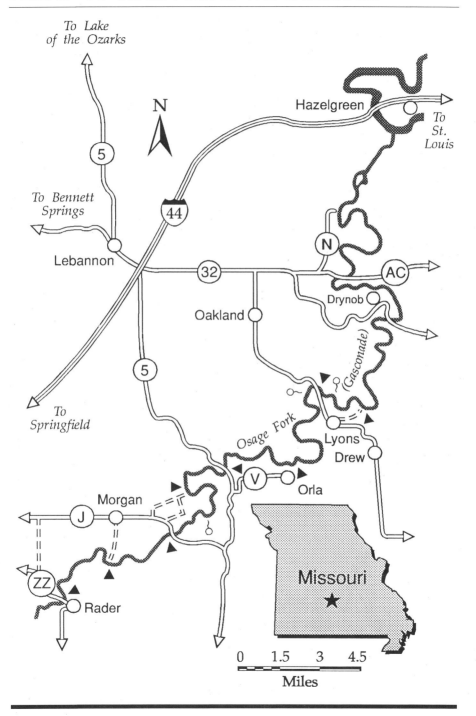

FLOAT 41 *POMME DE TERRE RIVER*

Region: Ozarks Border
Difficulty: I
Quadrangles: Cedar Vista, Cliquot, Elkton, Fristoe, Hermitage, Polk
County Maps: Hickory, Polk
Statistics: Drainage 828 sq. miles; Permanent Flow 99 miles
Put in: U.S. Army Corps of Engineers campground at the base of the Pomme de Terre dam
Take out: MDC Hermitage Access

The float: The Pomme de Terre River flows northward to the Osage River interrupted by two impoundments—Pomme de Terre Lake and Truman Lake. Long stretches of pools and swift, shallow riffles run between the dam at Pomme de Terre Lake and the town of Hermitage.

This is an excellent area to take the family. The canoeing is easy and the fishing is excellent for bluegills and crappie. These fish are easy for children to catch. You'll find bluegills and crappie along the weeds in the quiet pools and in the backwater areas. In the spring and summer, fish a live cricket below a bobber. Throw this rig next to weeds and logs.

Past Hermitage, you'll find lots of agricultural activity, development and swift water when both dams are running. Areas close to Truman can be treacherous.

Begin your float at the U.S. Army Corps of Engineers campground at the base of the Pomme de Terre dam where you find excellent parking. Take out at the MDC Hermitage Access which has an improved parking lot and concrete boat ramp.

For a longer float, continue on 6.6 miles to the Cross Timbers Public Use Area.

An MDC recreational value survey shows the Pomme de Terre River is very popular. It scored 7.1 on a scale of 1 to 10 for recreational value. And it ranked 15th out of 38 popular Missouri rivers and streams. But there are some problems. Survey respondents expect the recreational value to drop a few points because of intensive recreational use and shoreline development.

FLOAT 42 *ROARING RIVER*

Region: Ozarks
Difficulty: II and III
Quadrangles: Cassville
County Maps: Barry
Statistics: Drainage Area sixty-eight sq. miles; Permanent Flow 6.5 miles
Put in: Off County Road F past the restricted fly-fishing area
Take out: Highway 85 bridge at Eagle Rock
For more information: Roaring River State Park, call 417-847-2330.

The float: Roaring River is one of many tributaries of the huge White River system of the Missouri and Arkansas Ozarks. It is a small creek floatable in

FLOAT 41 POMME DE TERRE RIVER

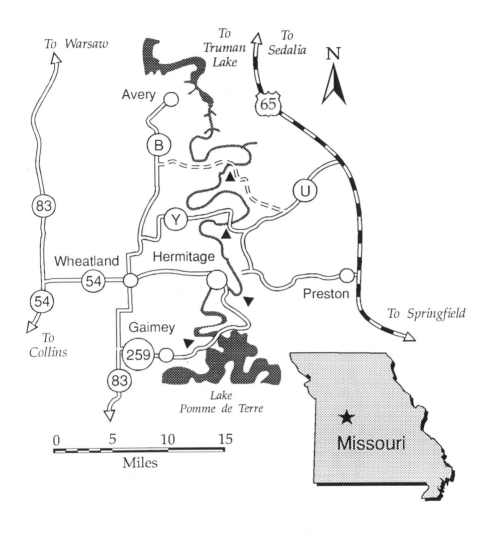

the spring. It offers a short, fast ride in high water. The gradient over the six-mile run to Table Rock Lake is fifteen-feet-per-mile. But best of all, the trout fishing is excellent here.

Roaring River begins at Roaring River State Park—one of the state's four trout parks. You can't float in the restricted fly-fishing area, but you can enjoy the fishing there before or after your run. This is a put-and-take fishery with a $2 daily tag and a five-fish limit.

Several streams flow through Missouri state parks offering developed camping facilities, including Roaring River State Park, Bennett Spring State Park, and Meramac State Park. Missouri Division of Tourism Photo.

FLOAT 42 *ROARING RIVER*

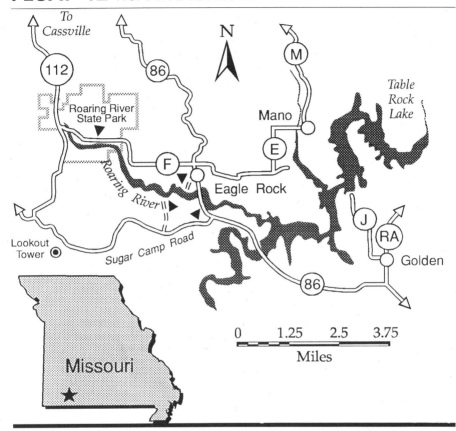

The 3,354-acre Roaring River State Park is an Ozarks geological showcase. Here you can see how the White River system cut the deep valleys from the Springfield Plateau forming the Ozark hills of this area. As you float, take note of the various layers of sediment that created the plateau: limestone, dolomite and chert.

Native Americans enjoyed this area, too, and used it as late as 1830.

In the park you'll see the Roaring River Spring that pumps more than twenty million gallons of water daily into Roaring River. There are ten miles of hiking trails, a campground, cabins and a restaurant.

Begin your float off County Road F past the restricted fly-fishing area. Follow state park fishing rules until you reach the MDC Roaring River Wildlife Area 1.5 miles downstream, then follow state regulations (see Appendix). Take out at the Highway 85 bridge at Eagle Rock.

This short run is less than six miles. When the water is up, the run is exciting. You should have no trouble catching a limit of trout for dinner either in the park or on your run.

FLOAT 43 *SHOAL CREEK*

Region: Ozarks
Difficulty: III
Quadrangles:
County Maps: Newton
Statistics: Drainage Area: 472 sq. miles; Permanent Flow 57.5 miles
Put in: County Road W across from Ritchey
Take out: MDC Cherry Corner Access Area

The float: Shoal Creek, which flows through Newton Country on its way to the Kansas border about thirty-eight miles west, is fast and fun for moderate and experienced canoeists. The average gradient is about six-feet-per-mile, with one stretch between Ritchey and Cherry Corner Access reaching a gradient of about eleven-feet-per-mile.

It's best to inspect each run before venturing into fast water. Shoal Creek has chutes, log jams and low-water dams—all dangerous—and it's best to consult a mile-by-mile resource book before running it. The best book is Missouri Ozark Waterways, published by the MDC (see Appendix).

Put in at the bridge on County Road W across from Ritchey. The MDC Cherry Corner Access Area is ten miles downstream. From this area it's another 4.4 miles to the Lime Kiln Dam and an MDC access. There are two low dams on this run. Use caution. From here it's a 9.6 mile run to the MDC Tipton Ford Access.

FLOAT 44 *SPRING RIVER*

Region: Ozarks
River: Spring River
Difficulty: II and III
Quadrangles: Joplin, Pittsburg, Sarcoxie, Stotts City
County Maps: Jasper, Lawrence
Statistics: Drainage Area: 1,160 sq. miles; Permanent Flow: sixty-eight miles
Put in: Talbot Wildlife Area MDC Access
Take out: MDC Larussel Access

The float: The Spring River is a lively stream, with an average gradient of five-feet-per-mile, flowing westward toward Kansas from the Springfield Plateau region. It cuts directly across a well-populated area near Carthage and Joplin.

To the west, the Spring River has some pleasant areas to float for the moderate-to-experienced canoeist. Toward the west there are problems with pollution (there are dioxin waste deposits in the watershed), agriculture, and development. The Spring River got a moderate 5.7 out of ten rating in the MDC's survey of recreational value with a rank of twenty-eight out of thirty-eight popular rivers and streams. The survey indicates that rank will drop in the coming years.

Big Spring feeds the Spring River ten million gallons of water a day. The

FLOAT 43 SHOAL CREEK

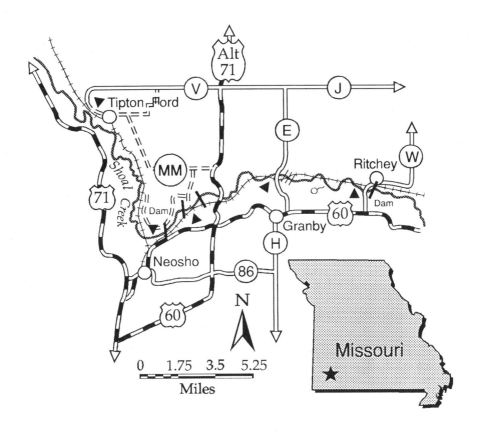

river is swift but slows down considerably as it reaches the Kansas border.

Put in at the Talbot Wildlife Area MDC Access about three miles from Stotts City. Take out at the MDC Larussel Access thirteen miles downstream. This is a tricky run. Watch for brush and log jams.

Kayakers race in the whitewater of the St. Francis. Missouri Division of Tourism Photo.

FLOAT 44 SPRING RIVER

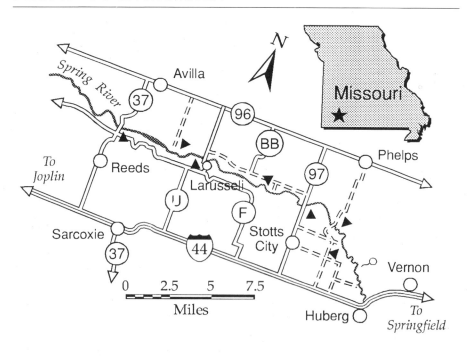

FLOAT 45 ST. FRANCIS RIVER/BIG CREEK

Region: Ozarks
Difficulty: II to IV
Quadrangles: Coldwater, Des Arc, Greenville, Fredericktown, Piedmont
County Maps: Iron, Madison, St. Francois, Wayne
Statistics: Drainage Area 1,135 sq. miles; Permanent Flow 180 miles
Put in: Whitewater - County Road H bridge near Syenite; For beginners - Sam A. Baker State Park on Highway 143
Take out: Whitewater - MDC Roselle Access at the Highway 72 bridge; for beginners - Highway 67 bridge
For more information: Sam A. Baker State Park, 314-856-4411; Mingo National Wildlife Refuge, 314-222-3589

The float: The St. Francis, and its major tributaries Big Creek and Little St. Francis, offer the wildest rides in Missouri. These are not streams for beginners. Instead, these streams offer the advanced canoeist a chance to experience whitewater similar to the western states. The average gradient is six-feet-per-mile.

If you aren't an expert, don't attempt to run the whitewater sections of these rivers. But do visit them and float the few gentle sections.

Here you'll find a unique rock form known locally as a shut-in. These are large, erosion-resistant rocks that form tight canyons in several sections of the St. Francis and Big Creek. Only experts can negotiate the waters in the shut-ins.

For whitewater enthusiasts, put in at the County Road H bridge near Syenite. Run the ten miles between here and the MDC Roselle Access at the Highway 72 bridge. This is a fast section with a twenty-feet-per-mile gradient. Past the Roselle access is an area of shut-ins and rapids covering about seven river miles. Only experts should venture beyond Roselle.

For beginners, put in at Sam A. Baker State Park on Highway 143. The next twelve miles to the Highway 67 bridge offers an easy float through the Mingo National Wildlife Refuge.

Sam A. Baker State Park makes an excellent base camp. You'll find camping, hiking and good fishing for bass, bluegill and crappie in the deep pools of Big Creek. The park also rents canoes.

The 21,676-acre Mingo National Wildlife Refuge has the largest area of hardwood swamp left in Missouri. There's a boardwalk nature trail though the area, but the best way to view the lowland wildlife is by canoe.

FLOAT 45 ST. FRANCIS RIVER/BIG CREEK

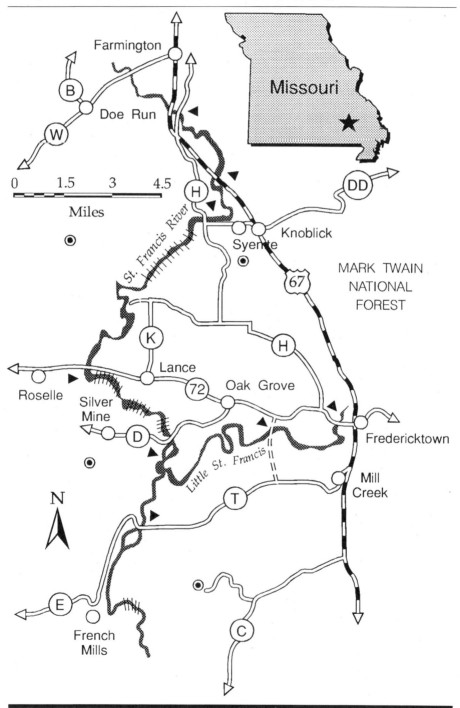

The St. Francis River offers some of Missouri's few stretches of whitewater. Missouri Division of Tourism Photo.

BIG RIVER REGION

When you cross the Missouri or Mississippi rivers today, you see muddy water flowing relentlessly to the Gulf of Mexico. If you're like most people, your mind is on bills to be paid, your job, the kids or some other daily grind. But what you're crossing when you drive that bridge is the history of great peoples dating back nearly 20,000 years.

We all learned in grade school that the Mississippi River at 2,348 miles long, is, after the Missouri, the second longest river in North America. Its triangular drainage area covers about forty percent of the country and includes all or part of thirty-one states, making it the third largest drainage in the world. The Mississippi means "father of waters" in the Algonquian language.

The Missouri was the southern boundary of the ice sheet of the last ice age. It's the largest tributary of the Mississippi River and originates at the junction of the Jefferson, Madison, and Gallatin rivers in southwestern Montana. The Missouri flows 2,714 miles to join the Mississippi. It is the longest river in the United States. We learned that Spanish, French, and later, American explorers used these rivers to discover the interior of this land. And, finally, settlers used them to travel to new lives in the far west.

Today we look down briefly as we cross some bridge and see barges chugging to some unknown destination. We see rock dikes and sandbars. We see scrubby banks and the broken-down vestiges of development. We see levees thrown up in a vain attempt to tame the two most powerful forces on the continent.

What we don't stop to consider is how these rivers looked before Europeans arrived. The two rivers used to meander over vast and fertile flood plains. Huge backwater areas provided homes for terrestrial animals and seasonal stops for migrating birds. Thick bottomland forests stretched to the bluffs and hid large mammals such as deer, bears and mountain lions.

These were the hunting grounds of prehistoric peoples. Beginning about 4,000 years ago, these people began settling the areas along the two rivers as their society changed from nomadic hunting to primitive agriculture.

Because of its central location and position at the confluence of these two great rivers, Missouri was the point of departure for western trails and expeditions. The Lewis and Clark expedition began near St. Louis in 1804. The Santa Fe Trail, which began at the Missouri River in Independence, was a trading route to the Southwest in 1821. The Oregon Trail, also beginning in Independence in the 1830s, was the route to the Northwest. Steamboat traffic on the Mississippi and Missouri rivers was the major form of transportation in the region by the 1820s.

The steamboats moved tons of everyday goods to ports in northwest Missouri and the Dakotas to feed the needs of settlers. Many of these boats sank in the treacherous waters of the Mississippi and Missouri. The Arabia sank near Kansas City and was discovered in 1989 buried in a soybean field about a mile from the modern river channel. You can see many of the goods recovered from that wreck at the Arabia Steamboat Museum on Kansas City's waterfront.

Today, the Mississippi River remains an important commercial artery—the Missouri less so.

There was a time when men set upon these rivers in canoes—Indians, fur trappers, explorers. People are again putting canoes into these rivers and paddling to find what once was here. You can still see remnants of the hardwood forests. You can still see the tall bluffs, the woolly islands and the abundant wildlife. You can still feel the weight of history pass by with the current.

FLOAT 46 *MISSISSIPPI RIVER*

Region: Big Rivers
Difficulty: I
Quadrangles: Foley, Hamburg, Winfield
County Maps: Lincoln
Statistics: Drainage Area at St. Louis 701,000 sq miles; Permanent Flow 498 miles
Put in: MDC Prairie Slough Access northeast of Elsberry off County Road P
Take out: Sandy Island Natural History Area

The float: If the thought of setting out on the Mississippi River in a canoe frightens you, it should. The river is dangerous. But that doesn't mean you can't float this giant safely.

FLOAT 46 MISSISSIPPI RIVER

Canoeing the big rivers is increasingly popular. Andy Cline Photo.

A group of paddlers canoeing through locks on the Mississippi River. Andy Cline Photo.

The Mississippi is large and powerful to be sure. As long as you avoid barge traffic, even a beginner can make this float.

Put in at the MDC Prairie Slough Access northeast of Elsberry off County Road P. Float about twenty miles to the Sandy Island Natural History Area two miles northeast of Winfield off Highway 79.

Along this route you'll discover numerous islands and mature forests. The islands make an excellent barrier between you and the main navigation channel where the barges run.

This is a one-day trip, but a vigorous one. There's a steady and relentless headwind on the Mississippi that all but counteracts the effect of the current. You can't float. You have to paddle.

Despite the few dangers and the strenuous paddling, this is an excellent trip and worth the effort.

FLOAT 47 *MISSOURI RIVER*

Region: Big River
Difficulty: I
Quadrangles: Langdon, Nemaha, Peru
County Maps: Atchison
Statistics: Drainage Area in Missouri 530,000 sq. miles, Permanent Flow 515 miles
Put in: MDC Watson Access Area off County Road BB near the mouth of the Nishnabotna River
Take out: MDC Hoot Owl Bend Access off County Road U near Langdon

The float: If you live in Kansas City or St. Louis, the Missouri River hardly seems suitable for floating. It's largely a huge, muddy channelized ditch. But when you get away from the cities, the Missouri has a different personality. It's not as wild as in the past, but you can still feel the weight of history pass by you in countless millions of gallons of water.

You'll see farm county, tall limestone bluffs, brushy islands, mature stands of sycamore and cottonwood. You'll also see the ravages of modern civilization, such as development in the flood plain, wing dikes, and the refuse of industrial civilization.

You can find some pleasant floating particularly in the northwest. Put in at the MDC Watson Access Area off County Road BB near the mouth of the Nishnabotna River. Float seventeen miles to the MDC Hoot Owl Bend Access off County Road U near Langdon.

You'll see many islands along this stretch. Because the Missouri still carries some barge traffic, it's best to float the secondary channels around the islands. This will add several miles to the trip. Expect to take two or three days if you plan to take an easy pace. You can make this trip in one day if you keep a brisk pace.

For a real adventure, put in at Watson and take out more than 540 miles later at the Lewis and Clark State Memorial Park on the Mississippi.

To learn about other sections of the Missouri, read *Exploring Missouri River Country*, published by the Missouri Department of Natural Resources (see appendix).

FLOAT 47 *MISSOURI RIVER*

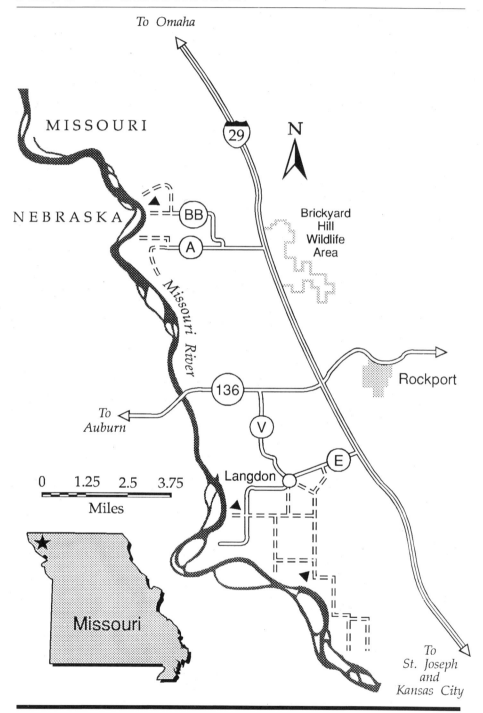

The backwaters behind the islands offer a sheltered route of canoeists and kayakers floating the big rivers. Andy Cline Photo.

MISSISSIPPI LOWLANDS REGION

When the first European explorers came though the Mississippi Lowlands, they discovered a vast area of hardwood swamps and fertile ground.

European exploration began when Father Jacques Marquette and the trader Louis Joliet traveled down the Mississippi in 1673. France claimed the Mississippi Valley in 1682 and named the territory Louisiana. The French established the first permanent settlement in Missouri at St. Genevieve in 1732.

Fur trading and lead mining fueled the French settlements before France ceded the region to Spain in 1762. The Spanish permitted settlement from east of the Mississippi. By 1800, most of the new settlers came from Kentucky and Tennessee. Spain ceded the region back to France in 1802. The French then sold Missouri and the rest of the Louisiana Territory to the United States in 1803.

The natural streams of the Mississippi Lowlands used to meander through mature hardwood swamps toward the big river. But cotton interests cleared the forests, built levees and ditches, and drained the swamps in the 1800s. The area swelled with plantations and slaves.

The effect is clear today. There are almost no natural streams left in the lowlands. Instead, they've been reduced to a series of ditches that move water from one point to another. The rape was so complete that the channelized streams no longer have names. They've been reduced to numbers.

While we can certainly mourn the loss of these streams, we can also enjoy something of what replaced them. Many of these ditches offer a unique floating and fishing experience.

Is it natural? No. Is it exciting? No. What it is, is different. Imagine paddling along a brushy corridor with levees sloping away from either side and a view miles long. It's the opposite of natural; it's high-tech. But the fishing is good for flathead catfish and crappie—two popular species.

Floating the ditches is not likely to become your favorite way to spend a day in a canoe. But it is worth a look to see to what extent man will go the change the environment. And you can't beat a mess of tasty crappie.

FLOAT 48 *DITCH #1*

Region: Mississippi Lowlands
Difficulty: I
Quadrangles: Bragg City, Deering, Hornersville, Kennett South
County Maps: Dunklin
Statistics: Drainage Area N/A; Permanent Flow 43.5 miles
Put in: Highway 164 bridge
Take out: MDC Hornersville Access off Highway 164 east of Hornersville

The float: A ditch? Well, yes. The streams of the Mississippi Lowlands have mostly been channelized out of existence to accommodate the agriculture industry. While it's certainly a great loss to treat a stream this way, what's emerged is a unique opportunity.

Ditch #1 is actually five ditches running parallel. You can access these ditches from highway bridges and the MDC Hornersville Access.

The water flows steadily southward in a surreal setting of brushy banks leading down long, straight corridors. People don't float this ditch for the scenery. They float it for the fishing. Despite the rape of a natural habitat, Ditch #1 supports good populations of flathead catfish and crappie.

For a short float, put in at the Highway 164 bridge and float 3 miles to the MDC Hornersville Access off Highway 164 east of Hornersville.

The current can be swift. But when it's slow you can base at one access and paddle upstream. To get from one ditch to another, paddle south of the Hornersville access to a junction route that connects the five ditches.

FLOAT 48 DITCH #1

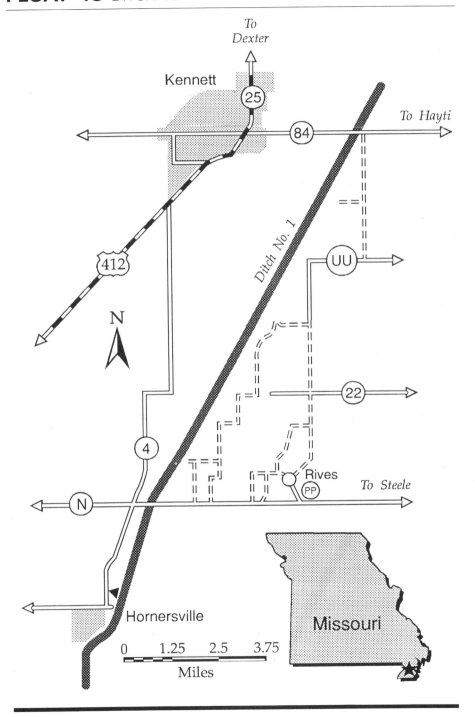

THE WATERSHED

John Muir once said everything is hitched to everything else. Streams are not just channels by which water travels to the sea. They are, instead, a part of a natural machine that works in a continuing circular motion. Part of that circle begins in the sky when water falls on the Earth as rain. The Earth soaks its share under ground. A plant draws its share from the ground and the air. The excess trickles downhill, gathering force with other trickles and spring seeps that become draws. These draws widen and join with other draws and springs to become streams. These streams become rivers and finally reach the ocean.

Between these trickles and seeps and the ocean is a complete world known as the watershed. Every inch of ground is part of a watershed. Each watershed has its main streams and rivers that drain the land. What happens on the land affects the entire watershed. If left in a natural state, the watershed functions normally. If disturbed, the degree of disturbance dictates the health and stability of the entire watershed—especially the stream.

In a healthy watershed, water flows with gravity gaining strength as it flows. It erodes loose rocks and sediments, but flows around the dense. The steeper the slope, or gradient, the faster the water flows and the more land it erodes as it forms a straight channel. As the gradient levels, the flow slows and the stream begins to meander.

This meandering scours outside bank, eroding it and forming a deep pool from the bottom sediments. These sediments collect in bars in the slower water on the inside channel bends.

As the system matures, the stream creates a pattern known to floaters as riffle-hole-run. The riffles are areas of steeper gradient where water flows shallow and swift. As the gradient levels out, the fast water cuts the bottom sediments creating a steep drop in the bottom—a deep hole with quiet water. From here the stream creates a run of smooth water flowing toward the next riffle.

These systems serve a purpose. Meandering keeps the stream from eroding the land. The riffle-hole-run system creates diverse communities of plants and animals.

A mature, natural stream has stable banks grown thick with willows and other woody plants. The forest above soaks up rain and snow-melt and keeps sediments from choking the stream. The water runs clear.

William Flick, in his paper The Living Stream, from The Stream Conservation Handbook edited by J. Michael Migel, identifies two distinct living communities within a stream—the fast-water community and the pool community.

The fast-water community, Flick says, is the greatest food-producing area of the stream. The fast water carries in nutrients, carries away wastes and replenishes oxygen.

In this community, the stream bottom is rocky and flat and the water is clear. Plants and animals here have adapted to life in fast water. Plants known as algae cling to rocks. This is the green stuff that makes rocks slippery when floaters try to wade through a riffle. Insects feed on this algae. They have adapted to life in fast water with claws and suckers that help then hold on to rocks as they graze on the algae.

Fish feed on these insects. You'll find trout in fast water. A trout's torpedo-like body allows it to fight the current easily. The sculpin, a small fish that feeds on insects, evolved a flat body that allows the current to flow easily over it while it clings to the bottom.

The pool community is a world of little current. The water is deeper, and usually stained. Here plants find soft sediment to take root. Small insects live in and around the plants and rocks, but they also float freely through the pool. Some insects and other animals bury themselves in the sediment. In the fast water, insects tend to feed on plants. In the pool, insects tend to feed on dead organic material.

Larger fish hunt among the plants and scavengers scour the bottom sediment. While larger trout feed or rest in deep holes, this environment is suited for the bass with its bulky body.

Terrestrial animals also use the pools. Birds and mammals catch fish and insects, feed on plants and drink the water. Disturbing the balance of one part of the stream and its communities will affect the entire stream. And it doesn't take a bulldozer, or an oil spill. Little things hurt, too. Here's an example:

I remember as fun times walking hand-in-hand with my grandmother to the stream near her home. In a paper sack we carried not our lunch, but the household garbage. Once there, we would heave the garbage into the flowing water. I'd watch it float away and think that was the end of that.

The idea was clear: a stream will float the problem away. I was too young to realize this practice harmed both the stream and its living creatures. The memory of those walks is still pleasant, but what we did makes me shudder.

Unfortunately, many people still think of streams and rivers as spillways to float garbage, or ditches to move water, or nuisances to high-yield farming, or a pipeline for chemical wastes, or a good place to drive an ATV. A stream is none of these things.

Streams in Missouri are under assault. To list and explain all those assaults would take more pages than are in this book. Luckily, two of the worst problems are ones floaters can do something about—clear-cutting the watershed's trees and channelization by farmers and developers. Of all the assaults on streams, these two are the most common and the easiest to correct.

Cut the timber too close to the stream and what happens? With nothing left to soak up water, too much flows into the stream when it rains or snow melts. This increases the velocity of the stream which has a direct effect on erosion. As the stream erodes the land, it picks up silt that clouds the water and disturbs the natural systems in the fast-water and pool communities.

In the minds of farmers and developers who clear-cut the watershed in the first place, the stream has now caused a problem—erosion. So they channelize the stream—straightening it out, making a ditch of it. What was once a meandering stream is now a swift running, muddy ditch.

Pollute the land and what happens? Every outrage we commit against the land harms the water. If we dump harmful chemicals on the land it leeches into the water table and finds its way to the stream. Depending on the chemical, it may kill plants, animals or both outright. Or it may kill nothing right away but make the water unsafe for fishing or floating.

Spray too much fertilizer on the land, or dump raw sewage or farm-animal waste products, and what happens? These things will add too many nutrients to the water causing algae to bloom . . . then die. Decomposition robs the water of oxygen killing plants, insects and animals.

Why do these things happen? Ignorance mostly. Farmers are not enemies of the land, and developers don't have to be. They're just trying to make a living. But, in the past, many didn't understand that destroying a stream cost them money. The muddy water will literally wash away their land—their profits—as it washed away the life.

Today, farmers, developers and conservationists are wiser and working together. You can get involved. Through the Missouri Department of Conservation/Conservation Federation of Missouri Stream Team program, and national programs like Save Our Streams by the Izaak Walton League of America, you can make a difference. It's a big job. Missouri alone has 56,000 miles of stream.

The IWLA program is a simple way for both groups and individuals to become involved. As in the state program, streams and rivers, or segments thereof, are adopted, then monitored for problems. IWLA teaches those involved how to test for pollution and erosion problems, then helps them find solutions. Solutions can be anything from getting a group of local Boy Scouts to plant trees on a stream bank to checking a company's chemical discharge compliance with a state environmental agency.

It's a matter of both education and a little sweat. Although you may not own land by a stream, you can help educate those who do and provide the labor to get the job done. Stream care professionals suggest landowners follow these five steps to help preserve and repair our stream resources:

1- Keep a 100-foot corridor of trees along streams. In clear-cut areas, planting such species as ash, silver maple and sycamore will help restore the corridor.

2- Don't change the channel and keep heavy equipment and ATVs out of the stream bed.

3- Stabilize banks with proper methods. Groups can get involved by planting black willow stakes that will bloom, grow and eventually stabilize the bank. Laying rock rip rap will also help. Never use junked cars or household appliances for bank stabilization.

4- Practice good soil conservation on farmland, i.e. reduced tillage.

5- Carefully consider all development along the watershed.

These steps will help repair damaged streams and keep virgin streams from becoming lifeless ditches. In turn the wildlife will flourish. Smallmouth bass will once again hide in the pools waiting for your lure to pass by. Without stream care, the landowners lose, you lose.

You can help landowners learn and adopt these methods when you and your group adopts a stream. Call the MDC for information at 314-751-4115.

FISHING

You've got the canoe tied on top of the car and tons of gear stuffed in the trunk. Now don't forget the fishing pole. Missouri's streams offer some of the finest fishing action in the Midwest. Cool, clear Ozark streams are home to rainbow and German brown trout, smallmouth bass, goggle eye and bluegill. The lazier, turbid streams of the north hold catfish, crappie, largemouth bass and walleye.

You'd think all that moving water would make stream fishing the domain of expert piscators. Not so. Stream fishing is actually one of the easiest kinds of fishing to learn because it's simple to find fish.

You can cast about a pond all day and not figure out where the fish live. You can motor for mile after mile on the large Missouri impoundments and never get a bite. But one look at a stream and you know for certain where the fish live.

When you know where the fish live, catching them is a simple matter of applying the right lure or bait to the right spot.

Finding fish in streams

The characteristic that makes a stream different from a lake is the same thing that makes fish easy to find: current. Current influences everything a fish does—from where it lives to how it feeds.

Current also gives a stream its unique structure. Fast, shallow riffles flow into slow, deep holes which flow into runs which flow into riffles again. This pattern repeats itself mile after mile from the headwaters to the mouth.

Floaters navigate downstream according to riffle-hole-run pattern. Fish use the same pattern to find a place to live, a place to eat, and a place to reproduce. Fish use current (or current dictates their behavior) in several ways. Actively feeding fish swim about in the fast current hunting food. Less active fish, or fish not suited to fast current, hide in ambush behind obstructions or in eddies waiting for food to float by. Resting fish hide in or behind current breaks such as deep holes, log jams, large rocks or fallen trees.

Current breaks such as large rocks and fallen trees are called cover. Fish use cover to rest, ambush prey and hide from predators. A stream without cover is not likely to hold many fish.

Concentrate your efforts at holes and runs with plenty of cover. Fish of all kinds usually hold on the downstream side of cover facing the current. Anywhere you find a big rock, log jam, grass bed or fallen tree in a hole or run, you've found a good home for fish.

Equipment for stream fishing

While it's quite possible to catch trophy-size smallmouth bass, catfish and trout in many Missouri streams, you don't need heavy gear. Think light.

A good outfit for the float angler includes at six- to seven-foot light-action spinning rod, a light-action spinning reel, and four- to six-pound test monofilament line. With this outfit you can catch most anything that swims in a Missouri stream.

Graphite rods are popular today. They are sensitive, light weight and respon-

A mess of fish means you can have a shore lunch—a tradition in the Ozarks. Andy Cline Photo.

sive. If you've had some angling experience, I recommend them. If you're a beginner, an inexpensive fiberglass rod will serve you better. Fiberglass is an excellent choice because it will shrug off the beating of the average float trip.

Select a small tackle box. You won't need a lot of hog-busting big lures for stream fishing. Instead, you'll need a careful selection of smaller lures, floats, hooks, split shot and other small items. I use a #3516 Phantom Jr. by Plano.

I enjoy fishing with live bait. So I also carry a small worm box—which is actually an extremely small styrofoam cooler—and a cricket cage. While you can use a wide variety of live baits, I found crickets and worms work well for just about every fish that swims in Missouri's streams.

Other handy items you'll need include: a small net for landing fish and a chain-type stringer for keeping fish to eat. Oh, and don't forget your fishing license.

Now let's take a look at the kinds of fish you'll fish.

Black Bass

Of the three black bass subspecies—largemouth, smallmouth and spotted—smallmouth and spotted bass are the two most common caught in Missouri's rivers and streams.

Black bass are the largest of Missouri's sunfish. In fact, they are not a true bass. The smallmouth and spotted bass are more streamlined fish suited to living in cool, flowing water. The largemouth is a bulky fish more suited to warm, still waters. Anglers find largemouth in the weedy backwaters of the big rivers and the major streams.

Spotted bass are the most versatile of the three. You will find them lurking in deep silty pools in northern streams and the cooler, clearer streams of the Ozarks. Good spotted bass streams include: the Osage River, Lamine River and Grand River.

Smallmouth prefer cool, clear, fast-running streams with rocky bottoms. Ozark streams noted for excellent smallmouth angling include: the Big Piney River, Current River, Eleven Point, St. Francis River, Gasconade, Meramec, and Niangua.

Bass anglers use a bewildering variety of live baits and artificial lures. The most popular live baits for stream fishing are worms, minnows and crawfish. The choice of artificial lures in almost endless. But it's best to stick with those baits that imitate worms, minnows and crawfish, such as plastic worms, crankbaits, and jigs.

Bluegills/Sunfish

The bluegill is popular with children. It's easy to find and easy to catch. Nearly all Missouri rivers and streams have good populations of bluegill. But you won't find them in the current. Look for them in shallow, weedy backwater areas.

Because bluegills have small mouths, don't use large hooks or big lures. A number six or eight hook with a worm or cricket will give you all the action you can handle.

Crappie

Crappie keep fishermen happy. They are easy to find, fun to catch and good to eat. Missouri anglers catch most of their crappie in the large reservoirs and in small community lakes and farm ponds. But floaters who explore river backwaters find plenty of fishing action, too.

There are two different subspecies of crappie in Missouri: the white and the black. They are similar in size and appearance. Despite their names, color is not a reliable way to tell them apart. The way to tell white from black is count the spines of the dorsal find. White crappie have six and blacks have seven or eight.

Black crappie prefer clearer water than do whites. If you float the big rivers, expect to catch white crappie. The most productive time for floaters to catch crappie is in the spring before the spawn, during the spawn and for a few weeks thereafter. Crappie move into shallow backwater areas as the water temperature reaches the sixties. The spawn normally begins for most of the population at or about sixty-eight degrees.

Crappie prefer to spawn in shallow woody and weedy cover along the banks of a backwater. Crappie eat small fish and aquatic insects. The two most popular baits are minnows and small jigs. Crappie also strike small spinners, crankbaits and topwater plugs.

There's plenty of excellent fishing on Missouri's rivers and streams. Missouri Division of Tourism Photo.

Goggle-eye

The goggle-eye, or rock bass, is a native of our clear Ozark streams. It's a feisty sunfish that bites readily, fights with vigor and tastes wonderful. The goggle-eye is easily identified by the bright red ring around its eyes.

Goggle-eye spend the daylight hours hiding among rocks, undercut banks or other cover in deep pools. It has the ability to change color to blend with its surroundings. As daylight turns to dusk, goggle-eye begin cruising for a meal.

Goggle-eye are easily caught with light-action gear and live bait such as worms, minnows, crickets and grubs. They will also bite such artificials as small jigs, spinners and crankbaits. You'll find good fishing for goggle-eye on the Black, Niangua, Jack's Fork, and Current rivers.

Channel Catfish

Channel catfish are a popular fish in Missouri—fun to catch and tasty to eat. They are a river and stream fish native to the Missouri and Mississippi River systems and drainages. Channel catfish live in the deep holes and backwaters. They feed mostly at night and mostly on the bottom. You might say channel cats are the street sweepers of the stream. They like their food old and smelly, hence the use of stinkbaits and other odorous concoctions to catch them.

You'll find channel cats throughout the state, but especially in the turbid northern streams that run through farm country, including the Nodaway, Platte, Grand and Salt rivers.

Flathead Catfish

The flathead is a big fish, a nasty fish. Unlike the channel cat, it is a predator. It likes fresh meat. It grows to sizes reaching forty-five pounds. It's all the fish you can handle on a rod and reel.

Successful anglers catch it with heavy line, big sinkers and live bait such as crawdads. You'll find the flathead brooding under logjams and in deep holes on the Missouri and Mississippi rivers.

Walleye

Some anglers say the walleye is the tastiest fish that swims. Maybe so. But the only way to find out is catch one...and you can find a bunch of them in some of Missouri's rivers and streams.

The walleye is a member of the perch family. It is a largely bottom-dwelling fish that feeds mostly at night. Walleye journey up the tributaries of major rivers and the creeks of reservoirs in early spring to spawn. Spawning begins as early as February and into April. You'll find walleye gathering on gravel bars in shallow water. You can catch them with small, white spinners and white jigs tipped with worms.

You can catch walleye in the spring, summer and fall in deep holes. Tip jigs with minnows or worms. Bounce these rigs on the bottom as you drift slowly over the hole. You'll find excellent walleye fishing in the Current, Black and Salt rivers, and in Mississippi River tributaries in the northeast.

Trout

Trout are not native to Missouri. Stocking programs began in the 1800s and continue today. Missouri now has a trout fishery that rivals the west. You'll find rainbow and German brown trout swimming in many cool, clear Ozark streams. The streams of the north are too turbid and warm to support trout.

Hatchery-reared trout released at the four Missouri trout parks are not selective feeders. They will bite just about any lure or bait they can get their mouths around. Offspring of these fish, however, are wild and difficult to catch.

Rainbow trout are mostly insect eaters and a favorite of fly fishermen. Brown trout are mostly fish eaters and fall prey to spinner and crankbaits. But there's hardly a trout in Missouri that can resist a worm or cricket.

Actively feeding trout cruise the fast riffles hunting food. You'll also find them lying in ambush in eddies and behind rocks and log jams. Excellent Ozark trout streams include: the Niangua, Current, North Fork, and Meramec rivers.

How to catch fish

There are two ways to fish a stream—wading or floating. Wade fishing is a fun way to take a break while floating. You don't need any fancy equipment like hip waders or a creel. Just slip on some old sneakers and walk into the stream.

Wading gives you two advantages. First, you can get a little closer to the cover you're fishing. Second, because you don't have to control a canoe, you can make many accurate casts near one piece of cover.

Fish hide behind cover facing upstream waiting for food to come floating by. If you're fishing on the downstream side of cover, you're fishing behind the fish. Present your lure or bait upstream and allow it to float slowly by the cover. This is what fish expect to see happen.

You can accomplish this by standing downstream and retrieving the lure toward you, or standing upstream and feeding the lure line as it floats away from you. Either way is acceptable, but beginners will find it easier to stand downstream.

If you don't want to get wet, stand on the bank across from the cover and cast at a forty-five degree angler upstream. Let your bait then flow downstream past the cover.

You can also catch fish while floating. This usually means the angler in the bow fishes while the floater in the stern controls the canoe. Two can fish easily from a canoe in still water.

It's difficult to fish close to cover from a moving canoe. But it's easier to drift fish from a canoe. My favorite tactic when drifting is to rig a live bait below a slip float (also known as a bobber). I simply pitch this rig to eddies, or submerged rocks and logs, and then allow the bait to drift with the canoe. I adjust the slip float so my bait hovers just a few inches off the bottom.

I believe the slip float rig with live bait is one of the best ways to catch any fish that swims in a stream. It's easy to rig, easy to fish and presents a live bait in a natural way. And it's an especially easy rig for beginners to cast.

A slip float rig is made with a slip bobber, a bobber stop, split shot for weight, a hook and bait.

To build the rig you insert the line into the center of the slip float. Tie a small piece of rubber band above the float with an overhand knot. This acts as the bobber stop. Tie on a hook and add up to three pieces of split shot below the float. Move the bobber stop up the line to the depth you want the bait to fall. Now you're ready to cast.

When the bait hits the water, the weight of the split shot makes it sink and the bobber stop then catches the float and stops your bait at the desired depth.

Sunfish are easy to catch when you cast a worm or cricket near aquatic weeds.

You can fish this rig in still water, fast water, close to cover, and even on the bottom.

What to do after the fish bites

Set the hook!

You'll now be glad you chose a long, light action rod. These rods make playing a fish—while standing in the creek or sitting in a canoe—easier. Keep your rod tip high and let the rod do the work. Keep the pressure on and soon you'll win the fight.

Catch and release fishing is a strong ethic today. But that doesn't mean it's unethical to keep a few fish to eat. You have every right to keep your legal limit.

But if you don't intend to eat your fish, please release them unharmed. Wet your hands before gently handling the fish. Remove the hook with a pair of needle nose pliers. Then gently put the fish back in the water.

APPENDIX

For more information

Floating in Missouri

Missouri Ozark Waterways
by Dr. Oscar "Oz" Hawksley
Missouri Department of Conservation
P.O. Box 180
Jefferson City, MO 65102

Canoeing in Northern Missouri
by Mary Ann Pemberton
Missouri Department of Natural Resources
This book is out of print. Check your local library.

Exploring Missouri River Country
by Don Pierce
Missouri Department of Natural Resources
P.O. Box 176
Jefferson City, MO 65102

Maps

State Topographic Maps

Department of Natural Resources
Maps and Publications
P.O. Box 250
Rolla, MO 65401
314-368-2125
7.5 minute quadrangles $2.50 each plus shipping

County Highway Maps

Missouri Highway and Transportation Department
P.O. Box 270
Jefferson City, MO 65102
314-751-2860
$.25 each or $25 for the entire set

State Map

Discover Outdoor Missouri
Missouri Department of Conservation
P.O. Box 180
Jefferson City, MO 65102
314-751-4115
This free map has the most complete list of MDC access areas, wildlife areas, natural areas and other public grounds.

Statewide Canoe Outfitters and Dealers

Adventure Sport Shop
427 Water St.
St. Charles, MO 63301
314-946-1180

Alpine Shop
601 E. Lockwood St.
St. Louis, MO 63119
314-962-7715

Backwood Equipment Company
3936 Broadway
Kansas City, MO 64111
816-531-0200

Marlin's Sport Shop
5408 Hampton Ave.
St. Louis, MO 63109
314-481-4681

Missouri Trails Outfitters
2707 Missouri Blvd.
Jefferson City, MO 65109
314-893-4004

Muddy River Outfitters
4307 Main St.
Kansas City, MO 64111
816-753-7093

Taum Sauk Wilderness Inc.
606 W. 48th St.
Kansas City, MO 64112
816-531-5580

Taum Sauk Wilderness Inc.
911 E. Broadway
Columbia, MO 65201
314-449-1023

Fishing Information

Missouri Department of Conservation
P.O. Box 180
Jefferson City, MO 65102
314-751-4115

Fishing in Missouri
A Special Section of the Missouri Conservationist
P.O. Box 180
Jefferson City, MO 65102
This free 32-page booklet outlines Missouri's major fish species, how to catch them, and lists access areas for 87 rivers and streams.

State Parks

Missouri Department of Natural Resources
P.O. Box 176
Jefferson City, MO 65102
314-368-2100

Missouri Tourism

Missouri Division of Tourism
P.O. Box 1055
Jefferson City, MO 65102
314-751-4133
Write for a free copy of The Missouri Travel Guide. It lists such attractions as: Bed & Breakfast Inns, Camping, Caves, Fairs, Golf, Fishing, Lakes, Music Shows, Rivers, Sports, State Parks, and Wineries.

Other helpful references

Geologic Wonders and Curiosities of Missouri
by Thomas R. Beveridge
Missouri Department of Natural Resources
P.O. Box 176
Jefferson City, MO 65102

The Terrestrial Natural Communities of Missouri
by Paul Weldon
The Missouri Natural Areas Committee
Contact either the MDC or the DNR

Streams for the Future
Reprint from The Missouri Conservationist
Missouri Department of Conservation
P.O. Box 180
Jefferson City, MO 65102

Out here–there's no one to ask directions

. . . except your **FALCON**GUIDE.

FALCONGUIDES is a series of recreation guidebooks designed to help you safely enjoy the great outdoors. Each title features up-to-date maps, photos, and detailed information on access, hazards, side trips, special attractions, and more. The 6 x 9" softcover format makes every book an ideal travel companion as you discover the scenic wonders around you.

FALCONGUIDES... leading the way!

Order today! Toll-free 1-800-582-2665
FREE catalog! No purchase necessary.

FALCON **P**RESS®   P.O. Box 1718, Helena, Montana 59624

243AP

FALCONGUIDES ★ *Starred titles are new in the* **FALCON**GUIDES *series.*

★ Angler's Guide to Alaska	$ 9.95
Angler's Guide to Montana *(revised)*	$10.95
★ Arizona Scenic Drives	$11.95
Back Country Byways	$ 9.95
Beartooth Fishing Guide	$ 7.95
Floater's Guide to Colorado	$11.95
★ Floater's Guide to Missouri	$ 9.95
Floater's Guide to Montana	$ 8.95
★ Hiker's Guide to Alaska	$ 9.95
★ Hiker's Guide to Alberta	$ 9.95
Hiker's Guide to Arizona *(revised)*	$ 9.95
Hiker's Guide to California *(revised)*	$11.95
Hiker's Guide to Colorado *(revised)*	$11.95
Hiker's Guide to Hot Springs	$ 9.95
Hiker's Guide to Idaho *(revised)*	$11.95
Hiker's Guide to Montana *(revised)*	$ 9.95
Hiker's Guide to Montana's Continental Divide Trail	$ 9.95
Hiker's Guide to Nevada	$ 9.95
Hiker's Guide to New Mexico	$ 9.95
★ Hiker's Guide to Oregon	$ 9.95
★ Hiker's Guide to Texas	$ 9.95
Hiker's Guide to Utah *(revised)*	$11.95
★ Hiker's Guide to Virginia	$ 9.95
Hiker's Guide to Washington	$11.95
★ Hiker's Guide to Wyoming	$ 9.95
Hunter's Guide to Montana	$ 9.95
Recreation Guide to California National Forests	$ 9.95
Rockhound's Guide to Montana *(revised)*	$ 9.95
Scenic Byways	$ 9.95
★ Scenic Byways II	$11.95
★ Trail of the Great Bear	$ 9.95

Falcon Press Publishing Co. • Call toll-free 1-800-582-2665